WHY IS MY CHILD'S
ADHD
NOT BETTER YET?

Recognizing the Undiagnosed Secondary Conditions

That May Be Affecting Your Child's Treatment

DAVID GOTTLIEB, PH.D.

THOMAS SHOAF, M.D.

RISA GRAFF, M.A., BCET

McGraw·Hill

New York   Chicago   San Francisco   Lisbon   London   Madrid   Mexico City
Milan   New Delhi   San Juan   Seoul   Singapore   Sydney   Toronto

The *McGraw·Hill* Companies

Library of Congress Cataloging-in-Publication Data

Gottlieb, David.
  Why is my child's ADHD not better yet? : recognizing the undiagnosed secondary conditions that may be affecting your child's treatment / David Gottlieb, Thomas Shoaf, and Risa Graff.
       p.   cm.
  Includes bibliographical references.
  ISBN 0-07-146221-X (alk. paper)
  1. Attention-deficit hyperactivity disorder—Complications—Popular works.
2. Manic depressive illness in children—Popular works.   3. Depression in children—Popular works.   I. Shoaf, Thomas.   II. Graff, Risa.   III. Title.

  RJ506.H9G68   2006
  618.92'8589—dc22   2005012264

1 2 3 4 5 6 7 8 9 0   DOC/DOC   0 9 8 7 6 5

ISBN 0-07-146221-X

Interior design by Think Design Group, LLC

McGraw-Hill books are available at special quantity discounts to use as premiums and sales promotions, or for use in corporate training programs. For more information, please write to the Director of Special Sales, Professional Publishing, McGraw-Hill, Two Penn Plaza, New York, NY 10121-2298. Or contact your local bookstore.

This book is printed on acid-free paper.

Contents

Preface

You have just asked your child to get ready for the fifth time. He finally seems to hear you, but instead of getting ready he screams at you to leave him alone. You insist, but your child continues to scream. You've had it: you struggle to get your child ready for school in the morning, then it is a fight to do homework, and at the end of the day he will not get ready for bed. During school, he is easily distracted and also has difficulty getting along with other children. In addition, he often makes up excuses for why he does not turn in his homework. The teacher thinks he needs an evaluation for special-education services. What is going on with your son? You feel like a failure as a parent and worry about your son's future. Your child's doctor thinks he has attention-deficit/hyperactivity disorder (ADHD), but your child has tried ADHD medications and does not seem significantly better. When ADHD medications do not seem to alleviate the symptoms, parents are often told to remember that "the medicine is not a cure-all" or "there will be problems even with the drug therapy." What should you do now?

ADHD is a common problem in childhood and adolescence: in fact, upward of 8 percent of the population has this psychological diagnosis. Though we'll go into far more detail about ADHD in Chapter 1, the generally accepted three core symptoms of ADHD are distractibility, impulsiveness, and hyperactive behavior. Most commonly treated with prescription drugs, ADHD has risen to greater prominence in the media as more and more families recognize the disorder in their children and seek treatment. But what happens when the child's condition does not improve with treatment? What can parents do when their child exhibits all of the symptoms of ADHD but does not respond in expected ways to medication?

Recent studies show that it is common for ADHD children and adolescents to have a second diagnosis—a coexisting psychological disorder—that interferes with the treatment of ADHD. The National Institute of Mental Health sponsored a large study of more than five hundred children with ADHD in the 1990s that showed that about 70 percent of children with ADHD have one or more additional disorders. This additional disorder needs to be treated in order for your child to improve. Without diagnosis and treatment, your child will not get better and may even get worse with standard ADHD medications. When additional diagnoses go untreated, your child is at risk for developing serious antisocial problems, such as drug abuse or criminal behavior, or developing serious mood disorders such as major depression or chronic bipolar illness. The sooner your child is correctly diagnosed and treated, the more likely you will be able to prevent the secondary problems from escalating.

This book will first help you determine if your child is receiving the appropriate treatment for his or her ADHD. Then it will help you determine which additional diagnosis your child might have. In addition, we explain how doctors and mental health professionals can treat these different disorders, and we offer information about what you can do at home and suggestions that you can give teachers to help your child at school. This book will help you coordinate what needs to be done for your child so that he or she does improve.

Upon further examination of these "complex" cases of ADHD, it becomes apparent that there can either be a coexisting mood disorder or a coexisting behavior disorder. Our book will explain the various mood disorders and behavior disorders that often occur with ADHD. For example, the ADHD child described at the beginning of the Preface exhibited angry outbursts with parents and classmates. These symptoms could be the sign of a mood disorder, like depression or bipolar illness, or the sign of a behavior disorder, like oppositional defiant disorder or conduct disorder, that is affecting this child *in addition to* his ADHD. It is critical to distinguish between a mood disorder and a behavior disorder because treatment of mood disorders is significantly different than the approach to behavior disorders. In addition, if the problem is a mood disorder, it is essential to determine which one it is, in order to treat the problem effectively. This book will explore these possible dual diagnoses in detail, offering you practical advice and coping mechanisms for dealing with these different disorders in your child.

Medications are one of the mainstays of treatment for ADHD, but prescribing medications can be tricky. For example, your child may be taking the wrong medication for the initial ADHD diagnosis. In addition, many medications for the second disorder sometimes react badly with medications used for ADHD, one interfering with the other or, worse, causing serious reactions and greater health complications. However, as we noted above, if the second disorder is untreated, it can exacerbate further the symptoms of ADHD, making it harder for the child to succeed in and out of school.

Why Is My Child's ADHD Not Better Yet? is a comprehensive guide to most dual diagnoses, not just the most common. Bipolar disorder and depression, two prevalent dual diagnoses, are covered first and in the most detail; they occur in about 20 percent of ADHD children. Bipolar disorder and depression are both types of mood disorders, but the strategies for treating each are quite different. Bipolar disorder has only recently been studied in children and adolescents, and, when it occurs with ADHD, it is an especially difficult disorder to treat. We outline psychological and educational strategies for you as well as your child's teachers, and we also offer medication advice. (In Chapter 4 we also explain what to do if your child has anxiety but is not depressed.) Next we distinguish the mood disorders from two other common dual diagnoses with ADHD: oppositional defiant disorder and conduct disorder. These are considered behavior disorders, and they occur in more than a third of children with ADHD.

Toward the end of the book, we delve into some other less frequent problems that can co-occur with ADHD. Tics and pervasive developmental disorder are two less frequently occurring diagnoses that can sometimes coexist with ADHD. Is there a reason why some ADHD children develop tics, and do stimulant medications make the tics worse? This book will offer suggestions for treating tics when they occur with ADHD.

Pervasive developmental disorder (PDD), traditionally known as autism, is now viewed as a spectrum of disorders ranging from autism to Asperger's disorder to PDD-NOS (pervasive developmental disorder, not otherwise specified). The basic underlying problem with PDD is difficulties with social relationships, communication, and changes in routine. The more serious cases, in which children hardly interact with others at all, are labeled autistic. Most psychological theories, including the current medical diagnostic manual *Diagnostic and Statistical Manual of Mental Disorders* (*DSM-IV*, 1994), suggest that children do not have both PDD and ADHD. However, we have found at a major treatment center in Chicago that if children show symptoms of both disorders, then their behavior improves if they are treated for both.

Two final areas of difficulty for some ADHD children and adolescents are sleep disorders and substance abuse. Parents have often mentioned to us that their ADHD children sometimes have trouble falling asleep or getting up on time for school. We will explain why sleep problems sometimes occur and what you can do to help. Problems with substance abuse can be even more frightening. These problems can range from cigarettes to alcohol and/or drug addictions. Why do some ADHD adolescents develop substance-abuse problems, and what can you, as parents, do to prevent this?

The suggestions in the book are based on successes we have had with our own patients. We are clinicians first and offer ideas that are practical for parents and other doctors. We have combined knowledge and expertise to offer you a complete "what-to-do" book for your child who may have another problem besides ADHD. In each chapter, Dr. Gottlieb, a psychologist, will first help you to discern if your child has a particular problem in addition to ADHD. He begins with case examples so that parents can get a feel for how children with each dual diagnosis behave. He will then outline the main features of the second diagnosis and show how it is different from ADHD. He will also explain how this additional problem can interact with ADHD to make it extremely difficult to treat. Dr. Gottlieb will then discuss psychological treatment strategies for the combined disorders. Dr. Thomas Shoaf, a psychiatrist and an expert on medications that are used for ADHD and for each dual diagnosis, will then discuss biological-treatment strategies used for your child. Where appropriate, he'll explain which medications to try first and how they work. We also review possible side effects of the currently used medicines. Then, Risa Graff, an educational therapist, along with Dr. Gottlieb, will offer you practical suggestions for common problems that these dual-diagnosis children face at home and in school.

We are well versed in research literature as well as clinical practice. Thus, we can offer you a complete and clear picture of the most up-to-date findings about how to help your children, without overloading you with extraneous or overly scientific information. Where there is research evidence to support an idea, the citations are given so that you can read more if you are interested in that subject. Where there is little research on some diagnoses, we offer ideas from our clinical work to help parents. For example, many of the ideas in the bipolar and autism areas are new, as there is little research about how these diagnoses interact with ADHD.

We believe that with ADHD and co-occurring disorders a combination of approaches works best. The problems are multifaceted, and so a multifaceted approach is more likely to lead to significant change. Treatments range from individual and family therapy to behavior-management strategies, educational interventions, and medication. This book is intended to help you understand your child's diagnoses and treatment options, as well as techniques that you can use to help reduce problems at home. The purpose of this book is to empower, so that you will know *all* of your options. *Why Is My Child's ADHD Not Better Yet?* is not intended to replace diagnosis and treatment by a professional, but to supplement such treatment. With this book, you will learn if your child has a problem that needs professional attention and what you can do to help.

Before we continue with Chapter 1, which is an introduction to ADHD, we want to reiterate the importance of not letting these coexisting disorders go undiagnosed. Begin treatment as early as possible because otherwise these problems are likely to be greater in adulthood. For example, adults with ADHD and behavior disorders may develop serious antisocial problems, such as criminal behavior and drug abuse. These very serious problems make it even more important that behavior problems are correctly diagnosed so that treatment can begin early, during childhood. Similarly, for mood disorders, it is also important that they be treated early. Manic symptoms, for example, often become more dangerous during adulthood. While a child in a manic stage may yell and throw things on the way to his or her room, an adult may get behind the wheel of a car when in a rage or may fly off to another city and spend thousands of dollars when angry with a spouse or boss. Also, depression, if not treated, has serious effects on a person's self-esteem and ability to learn. These effects are cumulative, so that the earlier the correct diagnosis is made, the sooner treatment can begin, and the sooner you can stop the damage to your child's self-esteem and learning.

Acknowledgments

Four years of writing, twenty years of seeing clients, and a lot of encouragement from our family and friends have led to the publication of our book. The support we received from our spouses Fawn Gottlieb, Robin Shoaf, and Lloyd Graff has kept us going. Fawn has read and reread the entire book countless times and is our in-house editor! Leslie Breed, our agent, has given us great advice about writing and marketing. Leslie saw the potential in our book, as did John Aherne, senior editor at McGraw-Hill. John has also been a terrific editor, offering many useful suggestions to make our writing clearer and more focused.

Along the way there have been a number of other people who offered advice and encouraged us. Writers Bonnie Rubin and Marla Paul helped us find our agent, and publishers Dr. Harvey Parker and Nancy Gray Paul made useful suggestions about topics to consider in our book. Carolyn Washburne edited our early chapters, and Professor Shelley Taylor offered support while we were searching for a publisher. Mike Able, Kurt Munson, and James Shedlock of Northwestern University Medical School Library helped us edit the references. Julia Anderson Bauer was our project editor at McGraw-Hill and helped us bring the book to publication.

We want to conclude by thanking our professors, our clients, and our children. Our professors helped us learn to think critically, our clients helped us formulate our ideas about multiple diagnoses, and our children helped us to become better listeners. While some of our clients' experiences have been used to illustrate the various diagnoses, we have withheld any identifying data in order to maintain confidentiality.

CHAPTER 1

What Is ADHD, and How Can a Parent Help a Child with ADHD?

Even when ADHD is the only diagnosis, standard medications are sometimes not very effective in treating it. The problem may either be that your child stops responding to the medications or that the medications may not help much because the child already has behavior patterns that are entrenched. Something more needs to be done.

Steven: The ADHD Medication Is Not Working

Steven is eight years old and has been on medication for ADHD for six months. Initially, there was great improvement on the medication: Steven listened more in class, did not misplace his work, and did not blurt out answers. However, lately all these symptoms have returned. Steven's parents do not want to increase his medication as he already experiences side effects on the current dose. Steven's appetite is decreased, and he has lost seven pounds over the last six months. What should his parents do?

Marilyn: Messiness and Foul Language Are Unchanged

Marilyn is twelve years old and has been taking medication for ADHD for nine months. While she is more focused in school, there has been no improvement in the disorganization of her room. There are papers, clothes, plates, pillows, and blankets all over the floor. Marilyn's parents tried to clean everything up for her a month ago, but within days the mess started building, and now they cannot walk into her room without stepping on things. They have tried reminding her and even yell at times that she should clean her room, but nothing changes. In addition, when her parents ask her to clean or do other chores, Marilyn sometimes swears at them. The disrespectful language is not used with other adults, just toward her parents, and it is used primarily when her parents remind her about her chores. Marilyn's parents have tried ignoring it and have tried talking and yelling, but she still uses foul language on a daily basis.

Defining ADHD

Before we explain what to do for difficult cases of ADHD, let's review what the diagnosis means. In the 1980s, there was one diagnostic category for any child with "distractibility problems," and that was attention deficit disorder (ADD). Then in 1994, the fourth edition of the *Diagnostic and Statistical Manual of Mental Disorders* (*DSM-IV*), which is the standard diagnostic text that mental-health professionals use, expanded the definition and listed three specific types of attention–deficit/hyperactivity disorder (ADHD): primarily inattentive type, primarily hyperactive-impulsive type, and combined type. The primarily inattentive person has difficulties listening, focusing on details, organizing, and remembering where he put things. In school, these children daydream at times and may not finish their work when the rest of their classmates do. Another common school problem for children with this type of ADHD is misplacing or forgetting where they put their homework papers.

An important point is that distractibility problems in these children are not constant. ADHD children and adolescents *do* pay attention sometimes. The problem is with "fluctuating" attention. In other words, children with ADHD, inattentive type, do not listen and focus at times. Clinicians have found that when children with ADHD are highly motivated in an area, they attend quite well. For example, some parents remark that their child is very attentive playing video games or while participating in a favorite class such as art or music. However, it is difficult for these children and adolescents to maintain their attention throughout the day on tasks of varying interest to them. While it is true that most of us have fluctuating attention to some degree during the day, the problem is more pronounced and more frequent for the child with ADHD. This distractibility causes problems at home and in school.

The person with the primarily hyperactive–impulsive type ADHD displays excessive extraneous movements, such as fidgeting, getting up, moving around often, and talking excessively. It is as if the person is always "on the go" (*DSM-IV*). Another characteristic of this type is impulsive behavior such as interrupting others and making comments without censoring inappropriate words first. The person "on the go" does not stop to think first if what he is doing or saying might intrude on other people's space. These children often appear rude or uncaring. However, it is important to remember that these ADHD children often have big hearts but are so impulsive at times that they inadvertently wind up offending others.

The combined ADHD shows characteristics of inattention and hyperactive–impulsive behavior. To be classified as combined type, according to the *DSM-IV*, there needs to be many characteristics of both types. People are not classified as combined if they only exhibit one characteristic of one type of ADHD. For example, Marilyn, who we introduced in the beginning of the chapter, was primarily inattentive, but she was sometimes impulsive in her use of foul language toward her parents. Notice that her swearing did not occur in all situations with her parents and never occurred at school. Because her impulsive swearing was occasional and because she did not exhibit excessive motor behavior, her ADHD would not be classified as the combined type. Her trouble paying attention in class and her disorganization are typical of the inattentive type of ADHD.

A new area of interest in the study of attention disorders is looking at the various cognitive processes that make up what we call "attention." What is the brain doing, for example, when we are "attending" to this paragraph of the book? First, our brains must perceive the words on this page, but at the same time block out, or reduce, the impact of other visual and auditory stimuli, such as the music being played in the next room. In addition, our brains must block other thoughts and worries we have, such as what we have to do the rest of the day. Furthermore, we sometimes have to switch back and forth from this book to a question one of our children is asking about homework. Selecting which piece of incoming information to focus on is an important aspect of attention. Cognitive psychologists call this selection process an "executive" function of the brain. Our brains are like corporate executives who must decide which piece of advice to focus on at any given point of time.

Notice that what we call "attention" is made up of several components: perceiving visual and auditory information, selecting which incoming information is more important to focus on, inhibiting other information, switching when necessary to focus on another source of information, and holding onto the information in one's mind so that it can be analyzed or stored as needed. When looked at this way, attention is really a complex task. Usually children with ADHD have problems in many aspects of attention. Currently researchers are looking more closely at the different aspects of attention that are affected in children with ADHD.

It is important to note that both children and adults can have this disorder. Twenty years ago it was thought that this problem was primarily a childhood disorder, and that many children were believed to outgrow the problem by adolescence or adulthood. In the last ten years, clinicians have realized that the disorder does not go away in adolescence or adulthood, but it may change its outward form. Adolescents and adults may not get up out of their seat and fidget incessantly, like some children would in school, for example. However, many adults continue to fidget at times and continue to be forgetful. In other words, their behavior changes somewhat because adults are more mature, have more self-control, and do not act the same as children. However, children with ADHD often grow into adults with ADHD.

Another question people sometimes have is whether an adult can develop ADHD. The problems do not suddenly appear in adulthood if they were not present before. However, distractibility and hyperactivity may have been present during childhood but not diagnosed as ADHD at that time. If a doctor takes a complete history, an adult patient who has ADHD will almost always give examples of either distractibility or hyperactivity as a child, beginning prior to age seven.

If your child or spouse is fidgety or forgetful one night (especially on the night you finish reading this chapter!), do not assume he or she has ADHD. In order for an accurate diagnosis to be made, there must be signs for at least six months. In addition, there must be indications of distractibility and/or hyperactivity in multiple settings. For example, if your spouse is distractible only when you are speaking to him, but never when he is speaking to his friends or coworkers, the problem is probably not ADHD! For a child, it is usually the case that there are distractibility problems at home *and* at school.

Neurobiology of ADHD

Most mental-health professionals agree that ADHD is largely a genetic disorder that tends to run in families. This does not mean that all, or even many, of the members of a family will necessarily have ADHD, but that some aunt, uncle, or grandparent, if not a parent, is likely to have had similar problems, whether or not they were officially diagnosed with the disorder. Remember that twenty or more years ago, people were not routinely screened for ADHD and instead may have been seen as lazy or as daydreamers. Genetic studies have shown that the child of a parent with ADHD has a 25 percent chance of having ADHD. The genetics of ADHD is not clearly understood but most likely is owing to the combined effects of numerous genes. The dopamine transporter gene (DAT1) and the dopamine 4 receptor gene (DRD4) may be associated with susceptibility to ADHD. Dopamine is an important naturally occurring chemical that transmits messages between cells in the brain. If the dopamine level is too low, it may be difficult for the child to pay attention. In addition to dopamine, another neurotransmitter, norepinephrine, may be deficient in patients with ADHD.

Let's look briefly at what structures of the brain may be affected in ADHD children. Research indicates that the prefrontal cortex, cerebellum, and basal ganglia may be smaller in children with ADHD. The prefrontal cortex is in the front of the brain and regulates attention: it inhibits processing of irrelevant stimuli (shutting out music while reading a book), sustains attention over long periods, and coordinates attention. The prefrontal cortex also facilitates socially appropriate behavior through its inhibition of inappropriate emotional responses, such as making rude remarks. Minor deficits in the prefrontal cortex would make it difficult for a child to sustain attention and to inhibit inappropriate behavior.

The cerebellum and basal ganglia are located toward the rear and base of the brain, and they help in the coordination of movement. One function of the basal ganglia, in simple terms, is to help keep quiet those muscles that are not needed for a particular movement. For example, when a person is sitting upright in a chair, the basal ganglia cells help keep the arms and legs still. When it is time to move, the cerebellum compares what a person thinks his muscles are doing with the position that they are actually in, and this helps him make the necessary corrections. Deficits in the basal ganglia and cerebellum would not only make it hard for a child to sit still but also affect the child's coordination.

Modern medical imaging techniques are helping to confirm current theories about what is happening in the brains of people with ADHD. Magnetic resonance imaging (MRI) shows that during attentional tasks (reading, quietly listening to a teacher), the activity in the prefrontal cortex of patients with ADHD is decreased. This decreased activity most likely is owing to a shortage of dopamine. In addition, another radiological procedure called positron emission tomography (PET) has demonstrated decreased frontal cerebral metabolism in adults with ADHD.

Medication Management of ADHD

The primary psychopharmacological treatment for ADHD is either to use one of the psychostimulant medications or to use a nonstimulant medication. The psychostimulants are methylphenidate (Ritalin, Metadate, Concerta), dexmethylphenidate (Focalin), dextroamphetamine combined with racemic amphetamine (Adderall), and dextroamphetamine (Dexedrine). The nonstimulant is atomoxetine (Strattera). All of these are approved by the FDA for use in children and adolescents. The stimulants have been studied for more than half a century and have produced the largest body of literature of any childhood psychiatric treatment. It is estimated that the stimulants help improve ADHD symptoms in 70 to 90 percent of children and adolescents (see Table 1.1 for details about dosages, mechanisms of action, and warnings). The stimulants cause the release of neurotransmitters, namely dopamine and norepinephrine, from nerve cells and also block their reuptake. These effects lead to an increase in dopamine and norepinephrine concentration at the receptors on the receiving nerve cells that in turn enhance the function of the prefrontal cortex. The medication atomoxetine, a nonstimulant, blocks the premature breakdown of the neurotransmitter norepinephrine, but it does not affect dopamine.

The medications for ADHD have been shown to improve a variety of symptoms: concentration, impulsivity, hyperactivity, aggression, defiance, working memory, handwriting, motor skills, peer relations, and awareness in sports. Through helping the brain

7

TABLE 1.1 Medications for Treatment of ADHD

Medication	Pediatric Dose	How Supplied	Mechanism of Action	Warnings	Common Side Effects
Atomoxetine (Strattera)	0.5–1.2 mg/kg/day, qam* or bid†	Capsules: 10, 18, 25, 40, 60 mg	Norepinephrine reuptake inhibitor	Metabolized by CYP2D6, so adjust dose for inhibitors of CYP2D6; check weight; severe liver injury	Indigestion, nausea, vomiting, fatigue, appetite decreased, dizziness, and mood swings
Dextroamphetamine (Dexedrine)	2.5–60 mg/day; divided bid†	Tablets: 5, 10 mg; sustained release capsules: 5, 10, 15 mg	Norepinephrine and dopamine reuptake inhibition	Check weight; avoid evening doses; use drug holidays if possible; caution if hypertension, cardiovascular disease, hyperthyroidism, glaucoma; drug abuse and dependence	Palpitations, tachycardia, elevation of blood pressure, psychosis, headache, insomnia, euphoria, dysphoria, restlessness, exacerbation of tics, dry mouth, weight loss, diarrhea, constipation
Dextroamphetamine and racemic amphetamine (Adderall and Adderall XR)	2.5–40 mg/day qam* or, for short-acting form, qam* and early afternoon	Extended release tablets: 5, 10, 15, 20, 25, 30 mg	Norepinephrine and dopamine reuptake inhibition	Check weight; avoid evening doses; use drug holidays if possible; drug abuse and dependence; caution if cardiovascular disease, hypertension, hyperthyroidism; glaucoma; psychosis; sudden death	Loss of appetite, abdominal pain, nausea, vomiting, fever, infection, insomnia, headache, dry mouth, weight loss, mood fluctuations, nervousness, and dizziness
Methylphenidate (Concerta, Ritalin, Ritalin LA, Metadate ER, Metadate CD)	5–60 mg/day for short-acting form; divided bid†/tid‡	Generic tablets: 5, 10, 20 mg; extended release tablets: Concerta, 18, 27, 36, 54, 72 mg; sustained release capsules: Ritalin LA, 20, 40, 60 mg; Metadate ER, 10, 20 mg; Metadate CD, 10, 20, 30 mg	Norepinephrine and dopamine reuptake inhibition	Check weight; avoid evening doses; use drug holidays if possible; may exacerbate tics; caution if drug dependence, hypertension, hyperthyroidism, seizures, psychosis, glaucoma, or cardiovascular disease	Decreased appetite, headache, nervousness, sleeplessness, and stomach pain

Drug	Dose	Tablets	Mechanism	Considerations	Side effects
Dexmethylphenidate (Focalin)	5–20 mg/day; divided bid†	Tablets: 2.5, 5, 10 mg Generic tablets: 1, 2 mg	Norepinephrine and dopamine reuptake inhibition	Check weight; avoid evening doses; use drug holidays if possible; may exacerbate tics; caution if drug dependence, hypertension, hyperthyroidism, seizures, psychosis, glaucoma, or cardiovascular disease	Decreased appetite, headache, nervousness, sleeplessness, and stomach pain
Guanfacine	0.5 mg tid‡	Generic tablets: 0.1, 0.2, 0.3 mg	Alpha 2 adrenergic agonism§	Sedation and hypotension	Dry mouth, drowsiness, dizziness, sedation, weakness, and fatigue
Clonidine	0.05–0.3 mg/day divided tid‡		Alpha 2 adrenergic agonism§	Sedation and hypotension; rebound hypertension may occur with sudden withdrawal	Dry mouth, drowsiness, dizziness, sedation, weakness, and fatigue

* morning dosing
† morning and evening dosing
‡ three times daily
§ combining with receptors to cause drug action

be more attentive, the medications can improve performance in many areas of a person's life. The medications do not permanently change the brain, though, and must continue to be taken in order for the child or adult to continue to do well. Sometimes the medications do not have to be taken everyday, however. If the ADHD symptoms are not severe and if the person is involved in an activity he truly likes, he may do well without medicine. This is why some parents do not administer medication to their child on weekends or holidays. It is important to note that this cannot be done for nonstimulants, like atomoxetine (Strattera), which need to be taken daily to be most effective.

Potential side effects of the psychostimulants include insomnia (50 percent), headaches and nausea (20 to 40 percent), irritable mood (10 percent), tics (less than 3 percent), and mild weight loss (33 percent). The side effects of atomoxetine include drowsiness (10 percent), nausea (20 percent), decreased appetite (16 percent), dizziness (6 percent), and mood swings or irritability (10 percent).

The side effects that parents and doctors encounter most with stimulants are insomnia and appetite suppression. Many of the sleep problems can be avoided by not administering the psychostimulants late in the day. If weight loss occurs, it is owing to the suppression of appetite or to an increase in metabolism. Appetite suppression is more likely to occur during lunchtime, especially when taking a once daily, long-acting stimulant. To address this concern, it may be helpful to increase the size of breakfast and dinner. If changing the meal routine does not help, then the dose of the medication should be decreased, or an alternative medication can be tried. Some of the longer-acting stimulants may last too long in the evening for children to have much of an appetite at dinnertime. In these cases, it may be helpful to switch to an ADHD medication that lasts only until late afternoon, rather than evening.

For the stimulants, the longer-acting form is generally given because the child does not need to take it repeatedly during the day. Longer-acting methylphenidate products include Concerta,

Metadate CD, and Ritalin LA. Longer-acting amphetamine is available as Adderall XR. These medicines last between six and twelve hours, depending on the type of medicine and the child's absorption rate.

Methylphenidate products are generally tried first because these are the most widely studied and have been used for almost fifty years. Either amphetamine (Adderall or Dexedrine) or a non-stimulant (Strattera) is tried next. Parents should be aware that there is a potential for the abuse of stimulants by some teenagers, and if this is a concern with your son or daughter, then you should monitor the number of pills used during the week. Methylphenidate and the amphetamines are carefully regulated by the Drug Enforcement Administration because of their abuse potential. Because amphetamines have a greater euphoric effect than methylphenidate, many experts believe the potential for abuse may be greater with amphetamines. In some cases, patients who have taken extremely high doses of amphetamines and then stopped them abruptly developed severe depression, fatigue, and sleep changes. Furthermore, chronic abuse can lead to psychosis, insomnia, irritability, hyperactivity, and personality changes. The least likely to be abused is atomoxetine (Strattera) because it is not a stimulant. However, this is a newer medication, and we do not know yet whether it will be as effective for as many children as stimulants are.

Here are a few other suggestions for children who take an amphetamine. Children should not drink a lot of orange juice in the morning, as ascorbic acid, or vitamin C, can decrease its absorption. Another interesting fact about amphetamine is that it not only increases dopamine and norepinephrine levels, but it also indirectly increases another transmitter, serotonin. This means that doctors need to consider the amount of amphetamine to prescribe if the child is taking any other medications that affect serotonin levels. Too much serotonin can lead to side effects such as dizziness, shivering, hyperthermia, or mania.

Lastly, for patients taking the amphetamine Adderall, the label indicates a warning about sudden deaths in children with structural heart defects. We do not know yet whether the risk is greater than for the average childhood population. According to FDA reports, sudden death is a rare occurrence, estimated at 5 per 1,000,000 patients taking Adderall. There are also rare reports of serious cardiovascular side effects of methylphenidate. The FDA continues to study the side effects of all the approved ADHD medications, and updates product labels periodically. Check with your child's doctor about any concerns you might have.

One other type of medication has been used in some cases to treat ADHD, namely the noradrenergic agents, such as clonidine and guanfacine. The Food and Drug Administration has not approved these medications, however, for indications other than hypertension, but they are sometimes used in conjunction with the stimulants for ADHD. Clonidine and guanfacine can help with aggression, hyperactivity, hyperarousal, and excitability by inhibiting the activity of the locus ceruleus, an area of the brain. These medications also enhance cognition and attention through receptors in the prefrontal cortex. The adverse effects of clonidine and guanfacine include dry mouth (40 percent), drowsiness (33 percent), dizziness (16 percent), sedation (10 percent), weakness (10 percent), and fatigue (4 percent). If clonidine is going to be stopped, it is important to taper clonidine rather than discontinue abruptly in order to prevent rebound hypertension. There have been rare cases reported to the FDA of children who died while taking clonidine combined with methylphenidate. Some of these children had cardiac abnormalities prior to taking these two medications. It is believed that these children died owing to reasons other than the medications, but there remains the possibility that the combination of clonidine and methylphenidate impaired their cardiovascular function.

What to Do When Medication Is Not Working

In the case of Steven, introduced at the beginning of the chapter, the amphetamine medication stopped working after a few months. The doctor did not want to raise the dose, as Steven already had side effects, namely a decrease in appetite. In a situation such as this, there are several alternatives. The first would be to try a non-stimulant like atomoxetine, or a different stimulant such as methylphenidate. In Steven's case, atomoxetine had already been tried and was ineffective in altering his ADHD symptoms. We decided to try a different stimulant methylphenidate. Often if a child develops a tolerance to one stimulant and it stops working, this is likely to happen with another stimulant. However, we made a few changes to the medication regimen in order to try to prevent this outcome. First, we recommended his parents only use the medication on school days—not on weekends, holidays, or vacations. Steven's problem was primarily distractibility in school. We wanted the medication to continue to be effective on school days and did not want him to develop a tolerance. The trade-off is that Steven was more hyperactive on the weekends, but his parents could deal with this by ignoring some behaviors and using behavior modification when necessary. (We will discuss behavior modification strategies in the next section.) To date, this medication approach is working. Steven's distractibility in school is controlled, and he has not developed a tolerance to the methylphenidate.

If your child does eventually develop a tolerance to all of the stimulants, another alternative would be to use a small amount of methylphenidate along with a small amount of a medication like risperidone. Risperidone may be added when there are ADHD symptoms of hyperactivity or impulsivity. This medication is not indicated if the problem is only inattention. Risperidone, and other atypical antipsychotics, will be discussed in Chapter 6 on medications for dual diagnoses. Another alternative, instead of risperidone, is to add a small amount of guanfacine or clonidine (see Table 1.1). The problem with guanfacine, clonidine, and risperidone is that there can be side effects. Owing to the possibility of serious cardiovascular problems that we mentioned earlier when clonidine is added to methylphenidate, doctors are more likely to add a medication like risperidone. One side effect of risperidone may be an increase in the child's weight. Furthermore, there are rare occasions where diabetes or tardive dyskinesia (an involuntary movement disorder, such as lip smacking, tongue protrusion, or movements of the fingers or limbs) has occurred. To minimize these risks, doctors prescribe a very small amount of risperidone combined with methylphenidate, and it has been effective in many cases where there is tolerance to methylphenidate alone. When a combination of medications is indicated, we recommend consulting with a child psychiatrist who is knowledgeable about drug interactions.

Most children do not develop a tolerance to the stimulants, so that combinations of medications are not needed. When only one medication is used, doctors sometimes do need to vary the dose in order to have the best possible outcome. Because ADHD symptoms are not always obvious in a doctor's office, it is important for teachers and parents to communicate with the child's physician so that an optimal dose is maintained over time. The goal is to help lessen the child's distractibility while not creating side effects. Sometimes we have to accept less than an ideal therapeutic response because we do not want the child to suffer side effects. When there are still some ADHD-related problems, behavior modification can be helpful.

Behavioral Treatment of ADHD

Generally, the optimal treatment for people who have ADHD is medication combined with behavior modification. Most studies show that medication works better than behavioral treatment alone, but behavior modification can be extremely useful to help parents target some of the child's bad habits that have developed owing to ADHD.

Behavioral treatments for ADHD can be useful to change habits at home or school, such as forgetting to do chores or not completing homework. Sometimes the medication helps the child focus so well on homework or chores that additional behavioral techniques are not needed; other times the medication helps with attention during school but is less effective after school. And sometimes, the child focuses better in school and at home but still forgets to fill out his assignment book or forgets to look at it once he comes home. While the great majority of children benefit from medication, in about half the cases we see in our offices there are still some behaviors that are not improved. Parents can devise immediate incentives and consequences for specific behaviors such as these. It is important that the incentive or consequence is something meaningful to the particular child, and this can sometimes be determined only by trial and error.

For example, in the case example of Marilyn, we worked on her use of foul language toward her parents. The parents determined that she swore at them an average of three times a day. This happened most often when she was asked to do some chore or join the family for dinner. We discussed this problem with Marilyn in a family session and offered an incentive if she cut down the inappropriate language to an average of one time or less per day. We decided not to ask for perfect compliance immediately, as we wanted to increase the chances we would have improvement in the coming weeks. The incentive was that she would earn one hour of her mother's time over the weekend to serve as a driver for her and her friends to go to the mall or wherever Marilyn wanted to go. Normally, I prefer a more immediate incentive each day, but we could not think of one that would motivate Marilyn. It is very important that the incentive be something that the child is excited about. It is also usually necessary to vary the incentive after several weeks so that the child does not become bored with it.

If there is no improvement after several weeks, parents should change the incentive or consequence. Often I will suggest using both an incentive and a consequence to make the behavior-modification plan more powerful. Possible consequences include losing phone and computer privileges for a twenty-four-hour period for older children, or losing video game and television privileges for younger children. If the behavior-modification plan is successful, there will be an improvement in the targeted behavior over a period of weeks or months. In Marilyn's case, after we achieved improvement over several weeks, we increased the expectation: she was no longer allowed to use any foul language toward her parents. After a period of time, the child is weaned from the incentive or consequence, unless the bad habit returns. Then the behavioral plan needs to be continued for a longer period.

Another useful technique is cuing by an adult. For example, the teacher can tap the child's shoulder in class when he or she seems to be daydreaming, or a parent can hold up a hand, or use a verbal cue like "take five" when a child's anger is escalating. These cues gently alert the child and may help her calm down before using inappropriate language. Teaching an alternative is also useful. For example, the child could go to a different room on her own for a couple of minutes to help settle herself. Thinking of a calming phrase, such as "it will work out in the end," may also help the child to be patient and keep perspective. However, any teaching should be done at a different time when the child is already calm, and not when a child's anger is escalating. There should be as little as possible said by the parent at that moment. We want the child to realize she will get less attention if her behavior escalates.

Another cognitive-behavioral strategy (a psychotherapeutic strategy to change a person's mental set, or way of thinking, in targeted situations) that often helps is to anticipate distractions that may occur in a given day and help the child to think about ways to avoid them. For example, if your child is often distracted in a certain class and forgets to turn in his homework, ask your child at breakfast how he can attend better today. Possible ideas include not sitting near someone he typically talks with, sitting near the front of the class, putting away all distracting books and papers, reminding himself as soon as he walks in the classroom "to stay focused today," or putting his homework in a particular folder so he will know where to look for it. Sometimes parents and teachers need to change the physical surroundings to help a child focus, such as allowing the child to take tests in a separate room where there is less noise. Usually it works best if the parents and teachers work together to come up with a united plan; then the child will be more likely to take the plan seriously.

Specific Suggestions to Help with Organization

Organization is often a problem with ADHD children. Organization requires focusing, reflecting, and planning, all of which are affected in ADHD. Time and patience will be needed by the adults working with these children. Here are some specific suggestions for parents to help their children with the organization of their bedrooms and their homework. The first problem mentioned below occurred with our earlier case example of Marilyn.

The Mess in Your School-Age Child's Bedroom Overwhelms You

There is no space to walk in the room without stepping on clothes, papers, or toys. Such disorganization is a very tough problem. Improving organizational skills requires parental forethought, energy, perseverance, and optimism. But the results are worth it! First of all, even though this is probably an issue that has frustrated you for a long time, it is important that your child perceive your interventions as loving help rather than as intrusions. As children get closer to adolescence, this kind of help gets much trickier to give.

Your child is not just a "messy child." He is unable to see the possible ways that a room or desk or a backpack can be organized. In fact, disorganization may feel natural to your child. Having clothes all over the floor, possessions strewn around the room, and food underfoot are just how things are in life for him. He probably does not relate problems with being late, losing homework, or missing toys to the way his room looks. Your child may not have a clue that visible boundaries in his room could make his life easier.

It usually seems clear to adults that socks go in a certain drawer and T-shirts in another, but to a child with organizational problems, these facts are not clear and/or seem unimportant. If you work with your child on the "mess" in his bedroom, he will probably find it very soothing once his bedroom space is under control.

To begin, take some time when your child is not at home to sit in his room and observe what kinds of things are kept in the room and where things are typically put—or dropped. Ask yourself the following questions:

- How many kinds of things are kept in this room?
- Would some of these things (such as toys, hobby materials, old school papers, or outgrown, but beloved, stuffed animals) be better off stored in a different place?
- Are the storage procedures obvious and easy?
- What bothers *you* the most about how the room is kept?
- What about the room's disorganization is most disruptive to your child?

Figuring out what is most disruptive or bothersome is very important, because you will need to identify specific goals and then prioritize them. Disorganization is a very stubborn issue. You and your child will see quicker success if you tackle only one or two specific issues at a time.

For example, if the biggest problem is having toys strewn across the floor, first tackle just that problem and ignore the others if you can. Disorganized children are often happier with "open storage" where they can see what they have and can see where to put things away. Your open storage might consist of plastic bins, laundry baskets, or shelves with plastic containers. While parents may prefer a less cluttered look, open storage is more likely to help your child stay organized. Many children like to have their containers labeled, while others prefer to throw stuff in as they choose. The bottom line is that you must make it easy to store the toys and easy for your child to locate those toys. If there are too many toys for your available storage system, pare down the inventory. Children who have problems with organizational skills are often visually overwhelmed. When they see too much stuff, they get overstimulated and are unable to organize it on their own.

It also helps to enlist your child in creating storage solutions. Take a trip to a store that has a variety of inexpensive containers and organizers. With your list of "things needing storage" in hand, wander the aisles with your child and try to imagine what toys (or clothes or other stuff) could go into various containers. Try to agree with many of your child's choices, even if they are outlandishly colored. The goal for this exercise is two-fold: to get your child more invested in the whole idea of storing things and to help your child feel empowered that he can make many of his own choices.

Another kind of open storage that children often like uses wall hooks or hooks put into a large piece of pegboard, like those used in tool shops or store displays. Wall hooks are great for quickly hanging up coats, sweaters, and hats. The smaller hooks on the pegboard can hold belts, jewelry, souvenirs, or the assortment of junk that often ends up piled on dressers and floors. If your goal is ease of putting things away and maintaining visible access (this helps your child!), a pegboard works wonders. A tip for younger children, ages four to about eight, is to read them *The Berenstain Bears and the Messy Room*. The book has great illustrations of an extremely messy room and uses practical solutions to clean it up.

Many children have problems putting away their clothes. Begin by analyzing whether your child has too many articles of clothing to fit easily into the space available. Crowded closets and overstuffed drawers make it very hard to keep things neat. For young children, put picture labels on the outsides of the drawers, so they can easily tell where their socks and pants go. If possible, have a clothes hamper or dirty laundry basket right in the room. You might want to start with one basic rule of putting dirty stuff into the place that has been designated for it. Remember that children who are disorganized probably won't be able to remember that their favorite jeans are folded under two other pairs of pants. You might want to experiment with rolling clothes and placing them side by side rather than folding them, so that your child's T-shirts or pajamas are all visible at once.

It is important for parents to remind themselves to:

1. Stick with one goal at a time
2. Provide frequent, loving feedback for the child's efforts to achieve his goal (at first, praise even approximations of achieving the goal)
3. Have natural consequences for good effort or for lack of effort toward the goal

Examples of natural consequences for lack of effort might be: toys on the floor get scooped up by the parents and put out of reach for a week; or, the time the parent spends cleaning the floor gets deducted from television time. Examples of positive consequences might be: five days of good effort earns the child a specific time for private parental attention; or, a cleaner room earns the chance to buy a poster or some other positive addition to the room.

It is also important to give yourself positive feedback—helping your child become organized is a difficult and energy-consuming task. When you feel your own energy is being used up, try to remember that you are helping your child not just with external (or environmental) organization, you are also helping him with internal organization, and that will help him feel a little calmer and more in control of himself.

Your Child Claims to Have No Homework, Forgets Assignments, or Doesn't Have the Proper Materials to Complete It

Homework is a major problem in many households, particularly when a student has attention problems, is disorganized, or has ups and downs in energy level and motivation. There are no easy solutions for these problems, but homework management will get easier if you can work as a team with your child and her teachers and if you remain persistent in your attempts to make changes. Teamwork in this case is critical. You will need to meet with your child's teachers and calmly describe how you see the homework problem from your end. Before your meeting, try to analyze where the homework communication breaks down by asking and answering the following questions: Does your child bring home an assignment book? Are the assignments written in the book? If the assignments are not written in the book, does your child know that there are assignments? Does your child know that there is an assignment but often forgets the books and handouts that are needed to complete assignments? Does your child ever lie to you about homework (usually this is when she claims that the work is done or there is no homework)? What kinds of feedback have you gotten from your child's teachers about homework? What kind of communication system do you think would help your child be successful in doing her homework?

When you get to the meeting with your child's teachers, try to calmly listen to their side of the homework situation. Even if you feel angry about what is happening to your child in school, it is crucial that you get the teacher invested in developing a homework strategy with you—otherwise it is extremely difficult to solve this problem. Most children who have problems knowing what the homework is do not write down the assignments anywhere, and this makes teachers feel frustrated and angry. They may need help seeing that simply using the assignment book is a goal itself and one that may require consistent direction and supervision from an adult in the classroom. Writing down assignments needs to become an entrenched habit. Ask your child's teacher what has worked for her in the past. Try to get the teacher to come up with a strategy that she can be comfortable with and that works for her teaching style, but you also must insist on consistency of supervision until you see consistency in the assignment book.

One of the most frequently used strategies is for both the teachers and the parents to initial the assignment book every night. This sounds fairly simple, but it may be asking a lot of the teacher, particularly if your child is in middle school and has many teachers to deal with. Some teachers are organized enough so that they know what the assignments will be for the entire week. If your child is lucky enough to have a teacher like this, you might ask for a note, an e-mail, or a voice-mail message with the assignments. This will enable you to check your child's assignment book and compare it to the expected assignments. But this should not replace the need for your child to learn to write down the assignments herself.

For young children in primary grades, it might work for the child to be matched with a buddy who is good at writing down the assignments. Your child can then compare her assignment book to her buddy's. This only works if your child is motivated and not embarrassed by the buddy system. The buddy system can also work well if the teacher has the entire class do it.

You may want to ask your child's school for an Individualized Educational Plan (IEP). An IEP will ensure that your child receives some extra services at school. Typically, an IEP is for special education services, such as meeting with a resource teacher or social worker. IEPs also can include classroom accommodations. (For more information about establishing an IEP, see www.ed.gov/parents/needs/special/iepguide/index.html or call the U.S. Department of Education's publication center at 877-4-ED-PUBS.) An alternative to an IEP is known as a 504 plan. This plan is for children who do not qualify for an IEP, but still need accommodations in their class, such as more time for tests. IEPs and 504 plans are mandated by law to provide for the special needs of students. ADHD is considered an impairment that can interfere with a child's education, and thus an ADHD student is eligible for one of these plans if it can help him learn better. The teacher, parent, and special-education support staff meet to determine if a plan is needed and to outline the goals and procedures to be used in school. We recommend that the plan be as specific as possible. It should take into account the teacher's style as well as your child's learning style.

If one of the goals is to improve homework completion, it is important to get the homework plan clearly written into this document. Don't let the IEP goal be something like, "Susie will write her assignments in her assignment book every day." This may be part of the goal, but the plan should include who will be directing, helping, and monitoring Susie as well. Younger students may also need assistance in packing their backpacks with the right books and materials. Older students should be taught to mark their assignment books with a simple code that reminds them which books to take out of their lockers at the end of the day.

After you and your child's teachers have come up with a written plan, you and your child should meet with the teachers again. The student needs to know—and may need to be reminded—that all of the adults involved have come up with a plan that is designed to enhance her learning and teach her very important skills. Unfortunately, children who are embarrassed by their lack of skills or who are trying to avoid being in trouble may try to manipulate the teacher or the parent by not always telling the truth about their homework situation. When the child knows that the adults "on her team" communicate often, this is less likely to happen.

Under even the best of circumstances, you will need some backup strategies. Your child should have the phone numbers of two classmates whom she can call to get the assignments for each class. Teach your child how to make these calls herself. You may need to listen in if your child has trouble writing down things while listening on the telephone. Some teachers do not mind the occasional call at home about assignments, but this should be avoided except in emergencies and done only when you have received prior permission. Ask your child's teachers how they would like you to communicate with them. Would they like to hear your concerns via e-mail, voicemail, a weekly note, a note only when you sense trouble, or an in-person meeting? Give your child's teachers choices, and then be persistent in communicating via the chosen method. You may also want to have your communication method and time structure (that is, how often you and the teacher will communicate) written into your child's IEP or 504 plan. Remember to give your child's teachers positive feedback about what is working for your child. Let them know how much you appreciate the extra time and attention they are giving her.

What should you do if your child knows what the assignment is but has left her books or handouts at school? First of all, try to have an extra set of textbooks at home. Many schools will put permission for an extra set of textbooks into your child's IEP or 504 plan. If you do not have an extra set of books, find out how late it is possible to go back into the school building. Many schools have custodians and/or late-working teachers who will let children back into the building up until dinnertime. Naturally, you don't want to make a habit of doing this, but if your child is motivated to do her work and wants to get the materials, going back to school is clear evidence that you truly value her learning and her compliance with the teacher's homework demands.

Improving homework communication skills is sometimes a long process. Set short-term and long-term goals for your child. A short-term goal might be: "Susie will write down her assignments for one week," or "Susie will have all her homework materials with her when she comes home from school for _____ days." Carefully monitor these goals and follow up with positive and negative consequences that are tailor-made to your child's needs and interests. Be sure to label all of the positive behaviors that you observe relating to your goals. Even if your child falls short of the goal, you can label and praise her positive attempts to reach her goal.

When Homework Is Done, Your Child Has Trouble Finding It and Getting It Turned In

If your child's backpack is a mess, assume that he does not know how to fix the problem himself. Think of your child's backpack as a traveling office that needs to contain the right papers and the right supplies. What the backpack needs to contain will vary greatly according to your child's grade level and the demands of his teachers. If your child has more than one teacher, and that is usually the case even in primary grades, you must find out whether the teacher has asked your child to keep his papers in a specific way. Once you know whether your child needs to use a three-ring binder, an accordion folder, or just a collection of folders and spiral notebooks, you can begin the process of teaching him how to keep all that stuff organized. Any of these devices can work, and, if your child's teachers are not specific in their demands, you can experiment to see what feels right to your child. The keys to all of these systems are organizing, labeling, and sorting frequently.

Your child will need to have places to put materials for each separate subject. And within each subject's "files," there will need to be a place for three kinds of papers: work to be done, work that is finished and needs to go to school, and work that is finished but can be saved in a separate folder at home. Sorting helps the child think about what kinds of papers are important and what kind of work has little or no value once he is finished with it. In addition, most students who have organizational difficulties rarely throw anything away; they will need help deciding which papers can be thrown away. Disorganized students tend to save everything and then feel overwhelmed by the masses of papers that are crunched into their lockers and their backpacks. Then they have trouble finding and turning in the homework they worked so hard to complete, which is why organizing these papers is so essential.

Assume that you need to teach paper sorting in a specific way. It is helpful to consistently do the sorting in the same place and in the same manner. For example, you might line up your child's folders horizontally across the kitchen table. The folders should be labeled in very clear, very large letters so your child can identify each one at a glance. If all of the papers for all subjects are mixed together, your first sorting goal will be just to separate them by subject. Sort the papers by labeling the subjects on big note cards and placing the note cards neatly across the table. Once they are separated by subject, you will sort each subject into four groups: work to be done, work that is finished and needs to be turned in at school, work that will be saved at home, and work that can be thrown away. For each subject, you will actually need two or three folders. A two-folder system works well if the folder that goes to school has two separate pockets, one for completed work and one for work to be done. The second folder stays home and holds those papers that you still think are important but do not have to be lugged back and forth to school every day. The same process of sorting can be done for three-ring binders and accordion folders. A binder or an accordion folder can have two sections for each subject just like the folders. You will still need to have folders or files for each subject's work that is saved at home.

You will need to start this project by being very involved in the decision-making process, but your goal is to gradually give your child all of the decision-making authority. Another important point is that the sorting must be done on a regular basis. It often helps to write "sorting day" or "backpack day" down on the family calendar and in your child's assignment book.

Even after your son's backpack has been sorted and systematized, he may still have difficulty putting everything in the right place in the backpack each night and may even forget to take it to school. It is helpful to have your child do his homework in the same place every day and keep his backpack there as well. Some children like to make a colorful checkmark in their assignment book as they put each finished assignment into the backpack. Other children benefit from having a large poster near their work space. The poster lists all the things that need to be in the backpack when they leave. Some families like to have the backpack put in front of the door that the child will be leaving by to go to school.

If your child struggles with organizational difficulties in general, organizing his backpack can be a great starting place to help him feel more in control of his surroundings. The sorting process is a critical skill to teach your child. Children also like to see that their parents need to sort their own stuff. When you sort things around your house, be sure to let your child know what you are doing by labeling it for him. Many children don't recognize that their parents do tasks that are similar to what children need to do for school.

CHAPTER 2

ADHD and Bipolar Disorder

The One-Two Punch

Your child or adolescent has been treated for ADHD, but the symptoms of distractibility, impulsivity, and hyperactive movement are still problematic at school and home even after months of treatment. Furthermore, the problems go beyond these three.

Alan: There Is an Explosion When "Highs" Are Punctured

Alan, age fifteen, was often on a "high." One evening at home, he talked excitedly about a new girlfriend and wanted to see her all weekend. Alan was pacing around the family room while he spoke, and his parents were seated and watching television. Alan exclaimed, "My girlfriend is the greatest person I have ever met. She is so wonderful." He had to see her and could not wait for the weekend to start. When his parents started to talk about the family's plans for the weekend and explained that he would not be free to see her that much, Alan got quite upset in a loud and animated way. His parents responded angrily, and Alan then swore at them, made a fist, and swung his arm toward the ceiling. He threatened to leave home or hurt himself if he couldn't see his girlfriend. He said that his parents were the worst parents in the world. Alan stormed into his room and turned on his stereo. His parents could hear him stomping around his room and swearing loud enough to be heard over the music.

The precipitant for the conflict could be different than seeing a new girlfriend. It could be plans to meet with friends to play a new video game or to participate in a weekend get-together playing music or some sports activity. Whatever the activity, Alan acts like it is the most important thing in the world, and it has to happen this day or weekend. He is excited and happy at first and then becomes angry and disagreeable if his parents impose any limits. His parents pay a price whether they impose limits or not. If they do not impose any limits, Alan may engage in potentially risky behavior, and if they do impose limits Alan may explode with rage. Alan's parents need to decide how risky or disruptive the proposed activity is, and whether it is worth the explosion they will have to deal with if they forbid or limit Alan's activity.

When Alan engaged in things that he liked doing, such as spending time with his girlfriend, he took risks and engaged in sexual behavior without worrying about the consequences. He confided in a friend and his therapist that he and his girlfriend were making wedding plans already. He talked about his friends thinking he was the most handsome boy in school and his girlfriend the most beautiful girl. However, a month later, not only were the wedding plans called off, but the relationship was over. When he could not convince his girlfriend to change her mind, there was a brief period when his mood became extremely deflated. He thought about suicide. Alan felt no one liked him and never would. The swing of emotions ranged from elation and excitement at one moment to despair at another.

It would not take much to set Alan off at school. Alan had difficulty paying attention and was often unprepared for class, leaving his books at home or in his locker. One day, Alan and his friends were tapping on their desks in science class. The teacher told them to stop, and Alan shouted an obscenity. The teacher then suspended him from class for two days. Alan kept his mouth shut at this point. He did not usually have a prolonged tantrum in school because he said, "My friends will think I'm crazy." Alan, like many adolescents, shows some restraint in school once clear limits are set.

Most people who encounter Alan remark how upbeat and energetic he seems. In most situations outside the family the teenager displays good humor. He is also quite talkative. He is often smiling as he talks excitedly about his day. His conversations can be quite colorful and entertaining. If adults show nonjudgmental interest in his remarks, Alan talks to others as if they were best friends and often relates personal information even though he may not know the adults very well.

Edward: Outbursts Get Physical

The same combination of overexcitement, risk taking, and extreme anger can be seen in preadolescent children. Usually the younger child is even more energetic and labile with frequent, often daily, outbursts of rage. For example, Edward was so excited when he came home from school that he threw his coat on the floor and raced to the television to play his new video game. While playing the game, he was extremely animated and yelled and cursed at the television. When the parents asked him to take a break to do his homework or to have dinner, he started screaming at them: "Leave me alone. I don't want to eat. Go away." When they insisted he stop the game, Edward threw himself and the game controller on the floor, and he cried or yelled as if they had just broken his leg. Talking to Edward at these times usually was ineffective, and the child's outburst sometimes escalated to throwing things or physically attacking his parents. It took quite a while, often an hour or more, before Edward settled down enough to join the family.

The same kind of outburst repeated itself at bedtime, when his parents insisted he stop what he was doing and get ready for bed. Edward's parents remarked that he wore them out by his repeated displays of rage, and, as a result, they made very few demands on

Edward simply to lessen the frequency of these problems. Another problem they had with Edward was that his risk taking was often exhibited in daredevil activities: for example, skateboarding or biking in places where there was a significant risk of falling. His parents remarked that they took more trips to the doctor or emergency room for Edward than they had done for all of their other children combined.

Edward had an extremely difficult time listening in school and was quite talkative even in situations that required quiet. He called out answers without raising his hand, walked around the room, and even began touching and poking others. Edward poked other people when he was bored and wanted to interact with them.

Henry: Highs and Lows, but Without Distractibility

Another child, Henry, age ten, had some, but not all, of the same problems as Edward. He showed signs of extreme mood fluctuations, such as getting very excited playing video games or going for a bike ride, or he would go into a rage if his parents impeded his plans. In school, if he was disciplined, he would storm out of the classroom.

One day his teacher faxed me a note when "Henry called another student 'gay' because she wouldn't throw a ball up the stairs to him. She was right not to do it, but he was frustrated. I told him that the language was inappropriate and that he should apologize. He wouldn't even stand by me and walked away. I called him back, and he began a tirade of, 'I don't want to talk about it. You always say it's my fault.' He went on, 'I can't sleep. I can't eat.' And then he walked out of the classroom." In this example, Henry was disrespectful toward his teacher. Furthermore, he escalated into talking about an unrelated subject: his difficulty sleeping and lack of appetite. His thinking had become tangential; that is, unrelated subjects intruded into his statements. All this went on in the classroom while other students looked on in surprise. His odd behavior became the source of teasing by peers for days to come.

Sometimes when he was disciplined for an impulsive comment during class, his mood would shift toward depression. Henry would become quiet and sullen. He would lay his head on his desk for an hour or more. One day he told another child that he was going to kill himself. The other child told the teacher, and the school social worker then contacted Henry's parents.

What was different about Henry, compared with the other child and adolescent cases we have been describing, was that he was not inattentive during class, nor was he disorganized. Henry showed signs of a bipolar mood disorder, but not ADHD, whereas Alan and Edward exhibited both and therefore could be diagnosed as having both bipolar disorder and ADHD. Sometimes Henry would get overexcited and impulsive, sometimes extremely angry, and sometimes depressed. These are hallmarks of bipolar disorder in children. Before looking more into the dual diagnosis of bipolar disorder and ADHD that existed in Alan and Edward, let us review what bipolar disorder is, and what characterizes this diagnosis.

Defining Bipolar Disorder

Adult bipolar disorder is described in the *Diagnostic and Statistical Manual of Mental Disorders* (*DSM-IV*) as a problem with mood, such that the person often experiences manic and depressive phases at different times. In fact, many refer to the problem as manic–depressive illness. The preferred terminology today is bipolar disorder: "bi" means two, and in this case it refers to the opposite ends of the mood continuum.

The *DSM-IV* lists the traditional criteria for the manic phase of bipolar disorder. The average age when a manic episode first occurs is in the early twenties, although it occasionally begins in adolescence, according to the *DSM-IV*. Mania is "a distinct period of abnormally and persistently elevated, expansive, or irritable mood, lasting at least one week." According to the *DSM-IV*, during the period of manic disturbance, three or four of the following criteria need to be present to a significant degree:

1. inflated self-esteem or grandiosity
2. decreased need for sleep
3. more talkative than usual
4. flight of ideas or the feeling that one's thoughts are racing along without letup
5. distractibility
6. increase in goal-directed activity (either socially, at work or school, or sexually) or psychomotor agitation
7. excessive involvement in pleasurable activities that have a high potential for painful consequences

The *DSM-IV* also explains that the disturbance must be present to a significant degree such that normal life activities are disrupted. In other words, if someone is excitable and shows even some of the above characteristics, but there are no problems in his relationships with family members, friends, or colleagues, and there are no problems with the day-to-day activities of life, then a diagnosis of mania would not be made.

According to the *DSM-IV*, in about half of adult cases, the manic phase of bipolar disorder is preceded or followed by a depressed phase. Even if there is not a depressive phase, the manic phase, lasting hours or days, is followed by a period of relative calm. This is still considered bipolar illness. The *DSM-IV* labels these kinds of mood disturbances, which are characterized by bouts of mania, as bipolar I disorder. Each of these moods could last for several days. These disorders are differentiated from bipolar II disorders in which the depressive phase of the illness is severe and the manic phase of the illness is relatively mild. The symptoms for this milder mania, called hypomania, are similar to those manic symptoms listed above but they do not "cause marked impairment in social or occupational functioning." Essentially, the manic phase is less extreme. The mental-health professionals who wrote *DSM-IV* in 1994 realized there were different degrees of manic disturbances in adults; however, they did not look into the range of disturbances found in children. Nowadays, mental-health professionals realize there is another type of manic disturbance seen in children.

Mania in Children

Recent research with children and adolescents by Barbara Geller and her colleagues indicated that three-quarters of the children and adolescents had rapid switching of moods, from manic to normal (or depressed), within a day. This "rapid cycling" is common in children who have mania, and less common in adults. In addition, for children and adolescents, the depressive phase is infrequent, whereas for adults, the depressive phase occurs about 50 percent of the time. In the case examples at the beginning of the chapter there were signs of rapid cycling. Manic or depressive episodes would usually last between thirty minutes and a few hours. Alan would explode in a rage if his plans to be with his girlfriend were questioned, and then an hour or two later he would be relatively calm. Edward, a younger child, would have a temper tantrum for thirty minutes if his video game was interrupted for dinner. Henry would have verbal outbursts in class if his teacher criticized his behavior, or he might put his head down on his desk and be unresponsive for a class period.

Besides rapid cycling, what else defines bipolar disorder in children? It is important to come up with defining characteristics that are separate from other childhood problems so that we have a clear idea of what bipolar disorder is like in children and adolescents. Geller and her colleagues studied in more detail the characteristics of the manic phase in children. They found several behaviors that distinguished mania in children from other disorders, like ADHD. Grandiosity and elated mood were found in 85 percent of bipolar children, whereas these are relatively absent from other disorders, including ADHD. Characteristics such as racing thoughts, hypersexuality, and decreased need for sleep were present in just under half of the bipolar children, and these were not present to a significant degree in problems like ADHD. There were also characteristics like daredevil acts and uninhibited people seeking that occurred in almost three-quarters of bipolar children, but these also occurred in one-fifth of children who have ADHD without bipolar illness.

In the three case examples at the beginning of the chapter, there were signs of grandiosity and elation. All the youngsters felt entitled to do what they wanted and were quite animated when doing so. Alan also exhibited preoccupation with sexual behaviors. Edward engaged in daredevil acts on his skateboard and bicycle and exhibited uninhibited people seeking, such as poking and touching others when he was bored.

Which behaviors are critical to the diagnosis of bipolar disorder in children? Daredevil behaviors are not by themselves indicative of bipolar illness because they can occur sometimes when there is only ADHD. Furthermore, hypersexuality is not a defining characteristic of bipolar disorder because it does not occur with younger children. However, grandiosity and elated mood are definitive qualities of mania in children. These occur in most bipolar children during the manic phase, but not in other disorders, like ADHD.

What exactly are "grandiosity" and "elated mood"? Grandiosity is believing oneself to be the best or greatest in some area, such as in school, sports, or dating. The individual thinks he is without equal. Because this is generally not consistent with reality (unless the person is truly a superstar like Michael Jordan!), the idea that one is superior in some way to other people is called "grandiose" thinking. It is normal, however, for children and adults to hold privately to some beliefs that they are special, or even great. For example, the author may think that he has a wonderful flair for writing. However, what distinguishes the writer's thoughts from a truly grandiose person is that the writer really knows that there are plenty of people who can write better than he can. Furthermore, the writer would not declare himself publicly to be the best, as many bipolar people do. Recall the example of the adolescent Alan, who thought he and his girlfriend were the best-looking people in his school. He did not feel there was any comparison and was happy to point out that fact to everyone!

The other hallmark of mania in children is "elated mood." This is more than being in a good mood. It is as if the person is on a high, and he exudes such happiness and excitement that other people cannot believe it. To others, it looks like an act: it makes others believe that it is inconceivable for the person to really feel that happy for so long. The mood can persist for hours or longer, sometimes until something disappoints the individual, in which case the feelings can switch quickly to rage. Otherwise the elated mood may persist until the person gets distracted or absorbed in some quieter activity. While Alan clearly showed signs of elation when he spent time with his girlfriend or even when he talked about her, it was less obvious that the younger children Edward and Henry were elated. Edward and Henry were very excited and animated when they were playing video games, but because younger children rarely talk about their feelings, it is hard to be sure they were "elated" in the same way adolescents, like Alan, talk about being elated.

My recent clinical work with bipolar children suggests that elation and grandiosity are not readily apparent with preadolescent children. One problem in determining the presence of "elation" and "grandiosity" is that they are subjective states, and most of these children do not talk about their inner feelings. Rather, the children act excited and appear "on the go" when they are in the "manic" phase. They act in whatever way they want to at the time. It is hard to stop them when they want to do something of their own choosing. Notice that this occurs when *they* want. These children are not always on the go, nor do they always disregard the feelings of others. It depends on their mood and interests at the time. Also, as they get older, they are more likely to want to please others, particularly their peers. Adolescents are better judges of when certain actions may meet the disapproval of peers and are more selective in their pleasure-seeking behavior. They may start giggling, telling jokes, or speaking loudly and rapidly at get-togethers with friends after school or at lunch, but usually they do not exhibit these behaviors during class. Some of their symptoms, in other words, may be suppressed by the desire to "fit in."

Alan, for example, did not want his friends and other students in the school to be angry with him. As an adolescent he had developed more awareness of his peers' feelings than the younger child Edward whom we described. Edward poked and touched others whenever he wanted stimulation, regardless of the feelings of his peers or teachers, something that Alan wouldn't dream of doing.

For the younger child, the problem is not that he is trying to be oppositional. Rather, the child is so revved up and excited that he "flies" through any stop signs put up by adults or peers. This behavior does not start when the child is supposed to be doing a chore or schoolwork, as is usually the case with oppositional children. It may start when the child, seemingly spontaneously, has the thought to poke or tickle his classmate, as in the case of Edward for example. He does so and continues when asked to stop. Edward wants an emotional interaction to meet his needs for excitement. When an adult intervenes, the child may poke him, shriek (or giggle), or run around the class. Sometimes the child does not stop until he is physically restrained. Ignoring this child's behavior is usually not effective in stopping it. When the child is restrained, he may either go limp, or he may start struggling and screaming. The latter is consistent with the description by some researchers of the lengthy "rage" reactions of some of these children.

So while "elation" might be the best term to describe mania in adults, it may not be the most accurate adjective for children. For example, while Edward's "out of control" behavior is traditionally called "elation," I prefer to describe the behavior as "impulsive pleasure seeking." This is more descriptive of the actual behavior of a bipolar child. The actual emotional state can vary: sometimes the child may seem elated, but at other times he is full of rage, particularly when adults interrupt his pleasure-seeking behavior. Repeated and impulsive behaviors designed to bring about pleasure are what parents and teachers observe with bipolar children. There is an intense, revved up quality in the way these children interact with others. If other people tolerate their behavior, these children seem happy and "elated"; however, often other people feel pushed too far by the bipolar child's antics and respond negatively. Then the child's mood changes from elation to rage. Although the emotion changes from elation to rage, the revved up quality and impulsivity remain the same. The child continues to act impulsively in his own interests during the manic phase. It is still considered mania, though the content of the child's emotional state, either giddy elation or intense anger, depends on how others react.

The other traditionally used term is "grandiosity," but I prefer the phrase "acting in one's own interests"—often without regard for others. "Acting in one's own interests" fits the behavior of a bipolar child better than "grandiosity," as the child does not necessarily act like he is better than others. A younger child may be self-centered, but not necessarily full of himself. In our examples, Edward and Henry acted in a self-centered way, but they did not express feelings of superiority. In the case of the adolescent Alan there were some signs that he thought he was superior ("I'm the best looking") as well as indications of self-centeredness ("I'm seeing my girlfriend no matter what you want"). Notice that self-centeredness does not mean that the child is selfish or uncaring all the time. However, in the manic stage the child is consumed with getting what he or she wants.

The key is that these children and adolescents during the manic phase are driven by their own goals and interests, and they act impulsively toward others in ways which heighten their own excitement or pleasure. Often their actions have to do with interacting with other people. The problem is that the other people may not want to be treated the way the bipolar child wants. The younger the child, the less likely he will take the time to check out what other people want to do.

In summary, both children and adolescents suffering from bipolar disorder are motivated by their own pleasure and often act quickly and impulsively to do what they deem pleasurable during the manic phase. With younger children, pleasure seeking often occurs to the point that the feelings of others are disregarded. Both children and adolescents sometimes react with extreme anger when they are prevented from carrying out their behaviors. During the course of a typical day, there is usually rapid cycling, such that the child alternates between pleasure-seeking behaviors, rage, relative calm, and, sometimes, depression.

Overlap with ADHD

Other symptoms like distractibility and impulsivity occur in many bipolar children but also are hallmarks of ADHD. Why not just diagnose these children as bipolar and leave out the ADHD diagnosis? Two researchers, Papolos and Papolos, argue that many of these children should be treated as having bipolar disorders, rather than the tendency of most professionals to diagnose only ADHD problems. While the Papoloses help point out the shortcomings of merely making an ADHD diagnosis, their emphasis on bipolar disorder could lead to making the opposite mistake: undertreating these children for ADHD. If the children meet the criteria for both disorders, the initial diagnosis ought to be a dual diagnosis. When treatment begins, and it usually begins with treatment for bipolar disorder, we can then see whether the child continues to show signs of ADHD even after the bipolar disorder has been treated. There is no way to tell for sure ahead of time. If ADHD characteristics like distractibility and impulsivity disappear once the bipolar illness is treated, then most clinicians would make a single diagnosis of bipolar mood disorder without ADHD. It is wise to consider all possibilities first and not rule out anything until treatment begins. Then we will not make the mistake of failing to diagnose and treat ADHD.

A careful history shows that in dual-diagnosis cases, distractibility and impulsivity are often evident in young children before other signs that are particular to bipolar illness. Researchers Biederman and Faraone indicate that ADHD-related problems with distractibility often occur when a child first enters school, before symptoms of bipolar illness are displayed. It is not clear yet why this is. It could be that ADHD manifests itself first, or that people are looking more for ADHD symptoms at a young age, rather than bipolar symptoms. Future studies will need to examine the age of onset of the defining characteristics of both disorders.

In addition, once the full-blown dual disorder is present, the degree of distractibility and impulsivity is more severe and pervasive than if the child only had one problem. For example, impulsivity for ADHD usually does not lead to daredevil acts like it does for bipolar children. Likewise, bipolar children without ADHD usually only have episodic impulsivity when they are in a manic phase. However, in dual-diagnosis cases, the impulsivity is usually persistent throughout the day and to a high degree. It does not occur only when the child is manic. Likewise, distractibility does not occur just when the child is in the manic phase. Furthermore, unless you treat both illnesses, the impulsivity and distractibility remain. A dual diagnosis captures the characteristics and treatment of the child better than a single diagnosis can.

This was the case for Edward, who was impulsive throughout the day as well as distractible during school. He would poke others or get up out of his seat frequently during the day. On the other hand, Henry would get in a rage *only* if disciplined, and though he was impulsive at times, he was not impulsive throughout the day. He also paid generally good attention in school if he was not angry or excited about an activity. Henry is a classic case of a child with bipolar disorder but not ADHD.

Clinical researchers like Biederman and Gied support the position that a dual diagnosis is needed in many cases. Gied notes that analyzing family history and examining brain-imaging studies may someday help doctors determine which children have both disorders. Family history often shows the occurrence of ADHD and mood problems like bipolar disorder in the family tree of one or both parents of children with dual diagnoses. However, children with only ADHD had family trees where ADHD was present, but bipolar illness was not. Brain-imaging studies are in their infancy for these disorders, but early reports indicate that the areas of the brain affected in bipolar disorder are different than the areas of the brain affected by ADHD.

The rate of ADHD in bipolar children and adolescents ranges from 30 percent in some studies to more than 90 percent in others. ADHD is more likely to be present in younger, prepubertal bipolar patients. While ADHD is prevalent in young bipolar cases, one would not expect in an average ADHD sample that there would be many cases with bipolar illness, because bipolar illness is a relatively rare phenomenon in the population. Yet, in several studies there were between 10 and 20 percent of ADHD children who also had bipolar illness. This is higher than most of us would expect. In part, this may be because the patients studied were from hospitals and university psychiatry clinics, and such patients likely had more severe problems than a community sample would. Still, the significant numbers of dual-diagnosis cases in major psychiatry clinics and hospitals helps support the importance of considering dual diagnoses when evaluating a child who at first glance seems to have only ADHD.

Treatment Strategies: How to Increase Self-Control

For bipolar disorder the most effective treatment is with medication. This subject will be covered in Chapter 6. Psychotherapeutic interventions are often used in conjunction with medications. Such therapy involves a combination of individual and family approaches. The aim of individual therapy is to help the child recognize the risks of his pleasure-seeking behaviors and to encourage the child to consider the consequences of his actions. The goal is for the child to display greater balance in his decision-making. Pleasure-seeking behavior would not be eliminated, but the risks would be considered more often, and this would lead to safer and more balanced behavior. Typical pleasure-seeking behaviors for adolescents would be drug use and sex, while for younger children the issue is often risky physical behaviors, like dangerous wrestling moves, skateboarding off hills, or climbing trees.

In dual-diagnosis cases, excessive risk taking and impulsivity are more frequent and severe than for one diagnosis alone, and thus it is difficult for the child to control these behaviors. The therapist and the parent need to be patient but persistent. The therapist must empathize with the difficultly the child has in controlling impulsivity; this is necessary in order to "keep an alliance" with the child. Keeping an alliance while also encouraging the child to evaluate and reconsider the degree of risk taking is a balancing act for the therapist. The therapist cannot become too didactic or critical of missteps. At the same time, therapy needs to be focused on risky and impulsive behaviors, as these are the crux of what is dangerous for the child.

For the older adolescent, the risky behaviors he talks about may involve sex and drinking. The therapist first listens and tries to understand the circumstances and what the adolescent's needs are. At the same time, the therapist wonders out loud how else the adolescent could meet some of his needs without taking on too much risk. For example, the therapist might remark: "You took a big chance there. I wonder how you could have had a good time and gotten everyone to have fun with you without drinking."

In the case of Alan, the adolescent we described at the beginning of the chapter, he talked about having unprotected sex with his girlfriend. He said that the odds were that she would not get pregnant. "Besides," he said, "I love her, and we'll get married if we get pregnant." Alan was just beginning high school and did not realize how hard it would be to support a child. Nor did he realize that getting married was unlikely at their ages. His exuberance about being with his girlfriend was greater than his common sense about sex and marriage. In other areas of his life where he was not so excited he showed better common sense. The goal of the therapist in this case was to build up his common sense in the area of sex and marriage. The therapist educated him about the risks of unprotected sex as well as the difficulties of having children when he was so young. The therapist pointed out that Alan could have fun—even sex—with his girlfriend without taking such huge risks. Alan considered the therapist's advice because there was good rapport between them and because the therapist helped Alan see that protecting himself would not ruin his having a good time. Bipolar and ADHD teens thirst for fun and excitement. The key for therapists—and parents—is to help them find a path that does not entail a huge risk as well.

It is harder for younger children to talk reflectively about their out-of-control behavior. When these children are in the office, they are often relatively calm and disinterested in talking about "manic" behavior that happened previously. Sometimes the therapist can point out the dangers in a caring way. For example, the therapist might remark: "Gee, you could have been hit by a car when you were skateboarding so fast down your street. Are there any skate parks near where you live, or do any of your friends have a cool ramp?" Another possible moment to make a brief, reflective comment about risks is when the child gets revved up playing a game in the therapist's office. When the child, in frustration, starts pushing a game board into the therapist's leg, the therapist might say: "Ouch. Do you really want to hurt me?" Another possible remark would be to comment on the child's overflowing excitement: "You are real excited about this game." If the child is calm enough to listen, you could add: "When you push too hard, I really feel like stopping. Maybe go a little easier on me." If nothing is getting through, sometimes the therapist might just say: "I need to take a break" and then pause until the child is a little less revved up.

In family therapy, risks are also discussed, and a behavior-modification approach is used so that there are incentives for safer behaviors as well as consequences for rules violations. For adolescents, rules such as curfew observance and control of dangerous substances are valued. Less danger is likely if the child is home on time and not abusing drugs; thus, these rules are often critical in family treatment. For younger children, completing homework and observance of bedtime rituals are often areas of conflict. Developing a regular routine with meaningful incentives and consequences often takes time to establish. Expect some outbursts at times, and be prepared to alter incentives and consequences when they become stale and ineffective.

Parents need to be realistic about reducing the frequency and severity of pleasure-seeking behavior. It is unlikely that all risky behaviors will be eliminated. The goal is to reduce the frequency of risky behaviors, and the behavior-modification strategy needs to take this into account. For example, it may be unrealistic to say that your adolescent is never allowed to be alone with his girl-friend. A more realistic objective would be to set a reasonable cur-few and to suggest settings where the abuse of substances is less likely. For a younger child, it would be unrealistic to say that he be in bed at the same time each night. Having a time range and also rewarding approximations to the goal in the beginning of treatment are important. If the goal for the younger child is to reduce physical aggressiveness in school, the teacher could send home a daily check sheet about the child's self-control, and the parent could use a favorite activity, such as use of the computer, as the after-school incentive. It may be unrealistic to control phys-ical and verbal behavior at the same time; thus, the initial goal is control of physical behavior.

In the case of the younger child, Edward, we first worked on his hitting and poking others. He would hit his parents or other children when he was extremely frustrated about not getting his way. The poking of other children in school occurred when he was bored. Edward's mother created a "control tower" at home and marked off sections every day that he did not hit or poke any-one. The teacher sent a sheet home each day to let the mother know whether he had shown self-control of his hands and feet in school. When Edward reached a certain level on his tower, he earned an exciting reward. The rewards generally involved fun activities with his parents. Once control over physical behavior was achieved, we worked on extreme verbal remarks, such as swears and cutting remarks. We used a similar behavior-modification sys-tem. The parents and therapist also suggested to Edward accept-able verbal remarks he could use when angry, such as "stop it" if another child was bothering him. At this time we did not worry about the tone of his voice, just that he used more appropriate words instead of swears and crass, cutting remarks.

How to Help with Schoolwork

Mania and ADHD are like a double whammy when it comes to concentrating in school or at home. Impulsivity and distractibility combined with mood fluctuations in children who have both diagnoses will make it hard for the child to focus in school and at home. Structure and support are needed in both settings. In school, it can be helpful to have an aide work with the student, particularly in classes where there is a lot of stimulation and opportunity for the student to get off track, or where there is a high level of frustration. Smaller class settings and a special study area may also be needed. At home, it is important there be a quiet, but not isolated, study area, so that the adult can monitor progress and help when the child is frustrated or bored. Again, it is important to be realistic in your goals. It is not likely that this child will finish all his work every day, but if there is movement toward this goal, it is important to acknowledge it and to consider incentives.

Before a child begins treatment for bipolar illness and ADHD, it is extremely difficult for parents and teachers to interest the child in academic work. The child is intense, emotional, and preoccupied with his own pleasure. How does the teacher or parent reach such a child? The child seems perpetually excited, either happily so or in an angry way. One option is to wait for the emotional excitement to wind down. However, this could take an hour or more. Another initial strategy is distraction. Try to engage the child in a calmer activity of mutual interest. If the goal is to have the child do a reading or math paper, start with flash cards or a game like Concentration, which gets the child reading and thinking. Then move on to the classroom work. Take turns reading parts of the assignment, as needed, to help him stay interested. This process will be described in detail in Chapter 3. This takes time and thinking for the adult and will work only some of the time. Another suggestion is to use incentives and consequences to help motivate the child to engage in a task of your choosing. For example, if your child likes to use the computer or play a card game, offer some computer or game time once he finishes an assignment. It will be helpful if you set a timer to cue him when he will need to stop playing the game. When the time is up, tell him you will reset the timer once he completes the next page of his class work. Remember that bipolar children prefer activities of their choosing, so that if they are going to do something a parent or teacher proposes it either has to be pretty stimulating or carry some important reward for them.

As the child matures, the parent or teacher may be able to label the revved up demeanor of the child, get him to identify it, and ask him to ease up on his "engine" if he can. This process is discussed in more detail in Chapter 3. Usually younger bipolar/ADHD children have trouble regulating their energy levels on their own. The younger the child, the more it is up to parents and teachers to notice when the child is escalating and to try distraction or incentives and consequences. It will be important, too, for adults to modulate the level of stimulation in the educational setting. In other words, a large class where there is a lot of stimulation would be difficult for these children. In addition, the work cannot be boring or overly challenging. If it is boring, the child will not find any interest in working, and if it is too challenging the child will experience frustration and rage. Look for warning signs that the child is beginning to "overheat," and try to intervene quickly. However, it is important for teachers and parents to realize they will not be able to anticipate their child's outbursts of pleasure or anger in many situations. Teachers and parents should not blame themselves. Teachers and parents may need to "tread water" until the medication and psychotherapy take hold.

In Edward's case, a smaller, more behaviorally focused classroom was needed for several years. There were clear rules and consequences, and teachers were more prepared to respond to "overheated" behaviors. We also tried using catchphrases, like "think about it" and "hold on," to cue him to slow down. These brief signals sometimes helped Edward to regain control, if he had not escalated too much already. Once he was running around the room or yelling at someone, cuing did not help, and teachers tried the best they could to bring Edward to a quiet, more isolated space in the school. It is easier to catch the child's aggressiveness at an early stage if the classroom is small or if there is an aide in the room.

Parents often hesitate to take their children out of traditional schools. However, you should look into options that may better meet your child's needs. A school setting that helps teach self-control is critical. These children may be bright, but they will not succeed in life if they do not learn self-control. It often takes a coordinated and sustained effort by parents, teachers, and doctors to help these children regulate themselves better. It also takes time! Medications often have to be titrated over time, and psychotherapy and behavioral interventions take time to be effective.

Other Goals of Psychotherapy

Another common goal of therapy is to increase compliance with the medication. These children need to take more medication than most ADHD children, because the medications for ADHD are different from the medications needed to treat bipolar disorder. Furthermore, the medications may have some side effects such as weight gain and a reduction in feelings of excitement. Even bipolar adults may go off their medications because they miss the "high" feeling they had without it—children and adolescents are no different. The dual-diagnosis adolescent may have received recognition from friends and other students for being funny and the life of the party. It may be difficult to tolerate some reduction in favorable peer feedback when the adolescent is regularly on his medication. Another compliance problem is that bipolar medications have to be carefully adjusted at times, and blood tests may be needed. The tests are an annoyance to many children and take up some of their free time. The child or adolescent needs to be continually reminded of the consequences of being off medication and needs to be complimented for his efforts to take the medications regularly. This is an important goal of psychotherapy. Parents can help the process go smoothly at home by being present at medication times to make sure their child or adolescent takes his medication if he has shown ambivalence about it. Try to pick a similar time every morning and evening when your child is not engrossed in another activity so that it becomes part of his routine. Keep reminders brief and calm. You may even bring the pill and water to the younger child if this helps make the process go smoothly in the beginning. Try to plan it so that something enjoyable, like television, computer time, or a favorite snack, begins after he takes the medicine.

When there is a depressive phase, it may happen suddenly and the parent and therapist need to be available to help the adolescent keep perspective. If your child experiences or perceives rejection from his friends, he may feel like a loser or even begin to feel suicidal. The therapist empathizes with the adolescent's pain but during the session also points out that there have been other times when the adolescent has felt accepted by peers and that this will happen again. During a future meeting, when the child is feeling positively about himself, the therapist tries to help the child anticipate that there will be some rejection and to recognize that his good traits are independent of what someone else happens to think at one moment in time.

Parents can help by also empathizing with their child's pain. You can say something like, "I can see why you are hurt by that." Do not try to rush your child to get over his pain. That would make him feel like you do not understand, and his pain would likely continue unabated then. Also, keep in mind that empathizing with his depression does not mean agreeing with any course of action he suggests. For example, if your teenager says he wants to fight someone, you could label and appreciate the underlying feeling of anger or say that it's okay to feel this way but not okay to act on the feelings in a violent way. If your child appreciates hugs, this might be a good time to offer a hug. Later that evening, if your child is still moping around, you might try to keep him company and offer an activity together, like a computer game, that might help distract him and keep his mind off the problem.

Dealing with Alan's depression was an important part of the therapy for him. When the girlfriend whom he thought he was going to marry broke up with him, he felt hopeless and suicidal. The therapist listened and showed that he cared about his loss, but he also gently pointed out how appealing Alan was to other girls. While he might not meet someone he liked as much as his girl-friend right away, the therapist was confident he would meet someone to date before too long. They also talked about how many girlfriends Alan had had over the last couple of years. Why would he suddenly stop attracting interesting girls now? The therapist tried to help the distraught adolescent to keep his perspective. This was an equally important task once a relationship with a girl was established again. At that time, the therapist reminded the teenager that sooner or later they may break up, similar to the previous relationship; however, the teen was told that he remains a wonderful and caring person, no matter whether he is currently having a relationship or not.

Another goal in therapy is to work on impulsive verbal remarks that can hinder the child or adolescent's acceptance by friends or adults. The child and therapist review how other people experience different comments and discuss alternatives that could accomplish the child's goal without turning off others. Often the issue is that the child has grown to like being funny and irreverent; however, the child does not recognize when it is excessive. The therapist can help the adolescent work on ways to monitor this, such as suggesting the adolescent look at other people's verbal and non-verbal cues. This is more likely to come up in therapy if the child recognizes that he has been rejected by someone; if he is not experiencing some rejection, the child is unlikely to be concerned with the nature of his verbal remarks. If your child says something at home that is irreverent or impulsive, and if your child is not over-heated emotionally, then you can reinforce the message that your child should consider an alternative. Keep it brief and light. For example, if your child called you "weird," you could say "how about 'old-fashioned' next time?" If parents try to say too much, it is likely to be experienced as criticism and provoke an angry response. The idea is to plant a seed gently if the opportunity arises.

Therapy is multifaceted and requires the coordination of therapist, psychiatrist, parents, school personnel, and the child himself. Because there are many upheavals in mood and behavior along the way, and because biological interventions do not always work fully or immediately, there needs to be patience on everyone's part. Psychotherapy involves individual and family therapy that are designed to increase self-control and to reduce risk-taking behaviors. Improvement will be gradual. There can be a tendency by any of the parties to give up, even though treatment is really making progress and just needs time to work more fully. One way to avoid this problem is to set reasonable goals and expectations from the start. In the next chapter, we offer some specific goals and solutions for problems that these children often experience in the home and at school.

CHAPTER 3

Children with ADHD and Bipolar Illness

Day-to-Day Problems and How to Deal with Them

This chapter will offer some concrete suggestions to parents to help with children who have both ADHD and bipolar illness. There are three basic areas that we will cover: how to help your child slow down and focus on everyday tasks, like bedtime and homework, how to help your child when he is extremely angry because his wishes have been frustrated, and how to reduce excessive risk-taking behaviors and grandiose thinking. All three areas are major hurdles for parents who are trying to help a child who is extremely impulsive and focused on his own pleasure.

When Your Child Is Revved Up

The first issue is to help your child to modulate his energy level so that he can attend to necessary life tasks at home and school. These children are typically so revved up much of the time that they have difficulty sticking with more deliberate tasks, like schoolwork and bedtime rituals. Often it is hard to get the children to slow down enough to start on these tasks. Even if they do get started, they are often in a rush and do a poor job, or they may get distracted partway through and then leave the task unfinished.

Your Child Is Revved Up at Bedtime, Refusing to Take a Bath and Playing a Video Game

The standard approach is to give a five-minute warning, and then a one-minute warning that it is almost time to stop. In addition, the parent would have developed a behavior-modification system such that the child already knows the incentives and consequences for getting ready for bed. The problem with this approach alone is that children with bipolar illness and ADHD are so excited and active that they may not pay attention to the warnings or the behavior-modification system that you have devised.

In this case, it is recommended that you engage the child in a "cooling down" activity. You meet the child halfway. Bedtime is put off temporarily, but the excitement of the video game is altered by switching to another game where you, rather than the computer game, control the tempo. An example may be shooting Nerf basketballs into a hoop with the child. "Let's see what you can do with the basketball. Show me your best three shots." This would be an example of how you might distract your child from the video game. Pick an activity your child enjoys, and one that allows her to show off in front of you. Most children have a hard time resisting the opportunity to display their skill in front of their parent. Once your child is engaged, you can gradually slow down the activity by stopping to praise the child and comment on her shooting style. No child can resist hearing talk about her skills, and while the child is listening, her "engines" are slowing down. The game goes on maybe ten minutes, or until you feel the child is ready to be "introduced" to the bedtime ritual.

The bedtime ritual consists of the activities necessary to get ready for bed, with a special story (the reward) planned for when the child gets into her bed. The ritual activities, like taking a bath and brushing teeth, require your presence, because the child is motivated to do these tasks owing to the interaction with you rather than the tasks themselves. While the child is in the bath, you can talk about the activity she just completed, like Nerf basketball, or talk about which story you are going to read in bed. If your child is not into stories, you might pick a short card game. If you can talk with the child, she is more likely to enjoy the interaction and at the same time begin to slow down. Remember if you are talking some of the time, she is listening (hopefully!), and listening is passive and quieting by nature, which will again help to cool those engines a bit.

Incidentally, once your child is slowed down, the potential bedtime reward is more likely to be of interest. The incentive, such as a bedtime story, will help you get your child to the final stage of lying down in bed. Some children need the parent to sit with them in the dark to slow down further and fall asleep. Be careful though about staying in the bed until they fall asleep. Children quickly become "addicted" to their parents' warm presence in the bed and will require your presence every time they go to sleep. It is better for you to sit in a chair nearby or leave with the words that you will check on her in five minutes to say good night. During those five minutes, the child continues to unwind, and is comforted by the fact that you are coming back. If necessary you can come back a couple of more times, but extend the time by five minutes each instance you leave. This way the child is getting less feedback from you and is more likely to fall asleep one of the times you leave.

It's Homework Time and Your Child Is Running Around Outside, Ignoring Your Requests to Come Inside

One approach is a variation of the above procedure for bedtime. When behavior-modification strategies, such as using rewards, are not working because the child is too wound up, try an intermediate activity that gives you some control of your child's energy level. The key idea is to help the child wind down. You might go outside and bring a ball to have a catch. While you are throwing the ball, comment on how well the child is doing. When you get the ball, hold it for a few seconds, as you talk about the activity, the dog, or something of interest to the two of you. If your child gets impatient, throw the ball back a little sooner. The trick is to find the rate of activity that sustains the child's attention but also slows him down somewhat. Sometimes it can take many minutes until the pace can be slowed. The length of time may be different on different days, depending on the degree of excitement of the child.

In order to help further with the transition to starting the homework, you may want to play a short card game next, a sedentary activity and a step closer to sitting quietly and concentrating on homework. At this point, you may be saying to yourself, this procedure takes a lot of work on your part, and that is true. Think of it as taming a wild stallion. Would you rather jump on too soon and get thrown off? For dealing with your child, the comparison of being "thrown off" might be a lengthy tantrum, which would take more time and frustration for all of you. Remember that your child has not yet learned how to modulate his energy level, and you are helping him do that. You are slowing the pace at a rate that depends on what is needed by your child that day. In other words, some days will be quicker than others.

Over time, the child will begin to internalize the "slowing down" process. You are teaching him a necessary coping skill that will have lifelong benefits. Before he can regularly use this skill, however, it will be necessary for your child to recognize that his emotional state needs adjusting. Most of these children do not realize how out of control they are acting. When he can observe that he is overexcited, he will then be in a position to try to regulate his own energy level. We will discuss the process of self-observation in the next section about homework.

Your Child Has Difficulty Focusing on Homework and Gets Up to See What Is Going on Around Her

You have tried to limit the distractions in your child's work environment. You have also chosen incentives and consequences to help motivate her to stay on task. But she still takes forever to do her homework, and she gets up repeatedly from her seat. What you need to do is to teach your child a cognitive strategy for focusing her attention on the homework. The first step in this cognitive process is self-awareness. This step requires the ability to look at oneself and develop verbal labels for one's own behavior. The ability to observe oneself is not easily taught, especially to preadolescent children. Here is an approach we use with younger children.

One way to build self-awareness is to use pictures or words to help your child recognize her emotional state. The labels progress from intense energy to a state of calm. You could choose one of the phrases in each of the following categories: (a) "revved up," "heated up," "hot," "red hot," "like fire"; (b) "slowing down," "warm," "lower flames," "orange hot"; or (c) "calm," "peaceful," "focused," "yellow hot." The idea is to teach the child to label her energy state and to recognize which state she is in when she is having a hard time focusing on her schoolwork. You might say, "Oh you're red hot, maybe that's why it is so hard to stay seated and do your homework right now." Or you could ask your child to pick the card that best describes her current state and then comment on your child's choice in a positive way. The purpose of this exercise is to build self-awareness, not necessarily to settle down the child.

Once your child can reliably label her energy state, you can move toward developing techniques with the child to help lower her energy to a level conducive to doing homework. These techniques could include any of the following: doing homework that is easier to handle in a revved up state, doing homework with more assistance from you when the child is in a revved up state, turning on music to help soothe or block out distracting noises, doing an alternate activity for up to half an hour until your child feels her energy level has lowered. Younger children will have difficulty choosing an approach, and you will need to recommend one that suits your child. These steps will probably take months, rather than weeks, to work on a reliable basis. However, do not be discouraged. This process is the essence of helping your child to control her emotional state. It is as important and time-consuming as teaching your child to read or do other important life skills. Your child's future success in school and in life tasks will improve dramatically if she can master these steps toward modulating her energy level.

Your Child Fails Tests Even When He Knows the Material

When your child fails several tests on content matter that you and his teacher know he has already mastered, it is important to analyze why he might not be able to demonstrate what he knows. Many children answer so impulsively on tests that they do not give themselves enough time to think about the question being asked. If they do process the question, they may not take enough time either to retrieve the answer from memory or to read all of the available multiple-choice questions. Even though a child really wants to do well, he may have trouble slowing his mind and body down to do optimal work. Working impulsively is a pattern that may take some time to change, but it is worth your time and effort because it will make your child feel better about himself, and it will generalize to other areas of his life. This problem can be particularly anxiety producing to parents when the test is being used to determine what reading group a child should be in or whether the child will be promoted to the next grade.

If your child is failing tests or not doing as well as he might because of impulsivity, it is very helpful to teach the child specific strategies for impulse control. Many children respond well to learning impulse-control strategies through playing games. Game playing has the advantages of being fun and providing opportunities for positive interactions with a caring adult. The game might be as simple as tic-tac-toe or as complex as chess. The bottom line is that it should be well within your child's capabilities, be enticing, and be an activity where it is obvious that a player does better when he takes his time. You should label your own waiting strategy by saying things like, "Wow, I really goofed last time [make a bad move at the start of the game]. This time I'm going to think first," or "I need to think," or "Let me take a good look so I can find my best move." Any time the child pauses to think, you should quickly and gently reinforce that behavior, but in a way that does not distract the child from the fun of the game. You might say something like "Good thinking" or "That pause really helped you." You might simply label this strategy as "the pause."

Once your child understands the benefit of pausing to think or to take a careful look at the game board, you can talk about what a helpful strategy these behaviors may be in real life. When the child is ready to do some homework, you can remind him of the thinking strategy that made him a champion game player. "Remember when you beat me at checkers because you were so careful with your moves. Let's try the same strategy with your math homework." Children who like to talk a lot may enjoy developing a verbal reminder to use on themselves before giving an answer. It should be a simple word or two so that it doesn't become its own distraction. Some children like to give themselves a nonverbal pausing cue. This might be touching a finger to their head or holding one finger in the air as if to say "wait a minute."

In order to help the child generalize the strategy to the school setting, you will need to enlist the child's teacher. Let the teacher know how you are working on changing your child's impulsivity in doing homework. Ask the teacher if she can set up some situations where your child will be obviously successful with the new strategy. Perhaps the teacher can give the child a short task in a setting where the teacher can provide a lot of attention (e.g., after school, in a room with an aide, or in the resource room). The teacher can then introduce the assignment by saying, "I know that your new thinking strategy is really going to help you with this assignment." The teacher may need to sit with the child to encourage and reward each instance of positive pausing.

The essence of this strategy is that you are conditioning your child to learn and use a new behavior pattern. It's also a strategy that has enormous power when the child can generalize it to social situations.

When Your Child Is Angry

The second problem area has to do with showing self-control when angry. All of us sometimes "lose it" when we are mad. But for the child with ADHD and bipolar illness, the threshold for explosive language or behavior is low. The child may scream or hit many times in a week. This behavior pattern needs to be changed in order for the child to attend traditional schools and participate in activities in the park district or community.

Your Child Yells at You in a Disrespectful Way When Asked a Question

Even a revved up child can learn to talk more respectfully to you. The first step is to decide with your spouse whether you are both ready to make this a priority. If your child is also hitting people when he does not like what they say or do, you will want to start with the hitting behavior first and move to the disrespectful language subsequently. Also, if you are going to be stressed out for the next month with problems at work or in the family, you will want to wait until you are both ready to work on the language issue.

Why am I warning you to wait until you are ready to tackle this problem? It will take a strong effort on your part for the first month (or more) to break a pattern of abusive language if your child has been exhibiting this behavior for a long time, as is the case for many children with bipolar illness and ADHD. When you are ready to start, the first step is for you and your spouse to decide together what you will consider "abusive" language and what alternatives will be acceptable. Then there has to be strict consequences and incentives for the child's use of language toward adults. Remember not to overload the child with new rules: pick a few abusive phrases to start, even if there are more, and ignore the others for now. You may want to start with the most offensive language, such as swear words or phrases like "you idiot." At the same time that you are preparing a behavior-modification strategy, it is still important to try to prevent "overheated" situations from occurring by distracting your child, if possible, when you sense he is beginning to lose it.

In conjunction with the behavior-modification strategy, we recommend using a cognitive strategy in which each person's needs or wishes are identified. It is the difference in people's wishes that usually leads to outbursts of anger and swearing. If you can tell that he is heating up, try to say out loud what is making your child angry before he starts to swear. You could say: "I know you want to continue playing, but I need you to stop for a little while because I have to drive the carpool." The verbal strategy of labeling the difference between what each of you wants may help your child keep his emotions in check. This strategy should be used if your child is only beginning to get angry, but will not be effective during a full-blown tantrum. Eventually, your child will hear these comments as "cues" that he needs to take a break.

When your child violates the standards for abusive language, the consequences and incentives at home must be short term but powerful. They need to be powerful because your child has to care about what you are doing, but this also means he will be upset when you impose the consequences. And you must impose the consequences regularly for the child to remember to control his hostile behavior. Initially, your imposition of the consequence, such as no television or computer for that night, will likely trigger a temper tantrum. Remember the analogy to a stallion. When the trainer first tries to tame the stallion, there is a powerful reaction by the horse. Your child likewise will not like the limits being set on his behavior. He is fairly self-centered and revved up and would much prefer for people to accept him the way he is. However, if you fail to act now, it will lead to serious social problems for your child down the road. It is important to set some standard that will help your child learn to modulate his anger at home because this will carry over to the way he handles anger and frustration in other settings, like school or after-school activities.

When you are ready to begin the behavior-modification strategy, explain to the child when he is calm what the new rules for respectful language will be and what the consequences will be. Be specific and only pick a few disrespectful comments to focus on first, like swearing or name calling. Be sure to suggest some acceptable verbal alternatives like "wait a minute" or "can I finish this?" By the way, if you offer "wait a minute" as an alternative, be sure to explain to your child that this cannot be used repeatedly to avoid listening to your requests. Also, explain what the incentives and consequences are going to be, and pick something you can enforce immediately for an hour or the rest of the night, depending on the severity of your child's abusive language. Possible consequences include loss of television or computer time or loss of phone or car privileges for older adolescents. For incentives, you can use activities like a trip to the park or a special game your child likes to play with you. For adolescents, the incentives might be that you will drive them somewhere, let them spend more time on the computer, or rent a game.

The child may say little when you explain this plan; furthermore, his behavior when angry is unlikely to change immediately. His swearing is so automatic when he is angry, that it may take weeks or more of consequences before he tries to control himself. If your child has a tantrum when you impose a consequence, try to ignore it unless he is destructive to himself or others. Your attention is likely to fan the flames of his anger. If you must intervene, keep it brief and to the point. Escort or carry the child to his room, if it is not possible for you to ignore him where he is. Rather than take the time to move the child, it may be easier for you to leave the scene. Also, if there are frequent tantrums, you can wait to impose a consequence later in the evening when he seems calmer and less likely to react with anger. Use as few words as possible, or use no words when you impose a consequence, just take an action: for example, taking away the computer's mouse lets your child know he has lost some computer time!

Another alternative for incentives is to place a star or sticker on a chart each day that your child has used respectful language with you. This way you can delay the actual incentive for a few days, which might be a trip to the park or ice cream store, or a special game you play together, such as playing catch in the backyard. The key here is to pick something special and exciting for the child. We want the child to be thinking about the reward and trying hard during the day to show self-control when angry. The younger child will need more immediate daily incentives initially, but after there have been a few weeks of improvement, try using stars to delay the rewards. If your child is earning the delayed reward 80 percent of the time over a few-week period, then you could broaden the definition of abusive language to include a couple more offensive phrases. Once you have achieved your goal for abusive language, you could try to delay the rewards for longer periods. Eventually, when you want to focus on a different area of self-control, other than control of abusive language, you can switch the rewards to the new area of concern.

Your Child Says "I Hate This" But Slowly Does What You Ask

The rule of thumb here is not to contradict your child if she is basically complying with your request. Let her blow off a little steam. However, recognize that her complaining is a signal that she is irritable at the moment or that she does not like the activity much. Keep your standards for the activity reasonable given her mood. This would not be the time to ask her to redo a project or assignment.

Some children with bipolar-induced irritable moods respond positively to comments of appreciation for their efforts, while other children when irritable react negatively to anything you might say. Use your judgment about whether to make a positive remark based on your experience with your child. In addition, when the activity is completed, consider suggesting a more pleasurable activity or taking a break. If your child is irritable no matter what you say, then wait and see what the child wants to do next. Again, your level of involvement will depend on your child's reaction to other people's remarks when she is irritable.

When Your Child Is Grandiose or Takes Excessive Risks

The third area of difficulty for these children is excessive risk taking and grandiosity. Problems here range from inappropriate touching by younger children to excessive drinking and sexual promiscuity by adolescents. The child or adolescent does not consider social norms but does what is exciting for himself in the moment. These children do not typically think about the consequences ahead of time.

Your Adolescent Comes Home Drunk Well Past His Curfew

As a parent your nightmare just occurred in real life. The only saving grace is that he has not also gotten into a dangerous car accident. What do you do? Not much while he is drunk and out of it. Tell him you will talk in the morning and help him get up to bed. Before you go to sleep, talk over with your spouse how you will both respond in the morning. The goal is to reduce dangerous, risk-taking activities. Think about what situations are most dangerous, and think about when and where they occur. If these activities are more likely to occur on the weekend, you want to focus your limit setting on this time period. If they are more likely to occur at someone's house, you will want to focus on this. Remember that you cannot follow your child around, nor can you eliminate all risk taking. You want to try to limit the most serious problems, and excessive drinking falls into that category.

In the morning, have a discussion with your adolescent first about where he was and what he was doing. Calmly, but seriously, explain the dangers of his excessive drinking. Let him know you will not tolerate this. As a start, for the next month, limit the time he spends at the place where this occurred. You are also going to impose a briefer, but more significant, consequence for his drinking and breaking curfew. The consequence may be being grounded for a few days or losing car privileges for a week. Generally the consequence should be brief but long enough to be meaningful. You can always reimpose the consequence for this or other risky behavior in the future.

While limiting the adolescent's presence at the house where the excessive drinking occurred will not stop him from drinking elsewhere, nor really stop him from going back to the house in question without your knowledge, it will put him on notice that you are determined to limit this behavior. The implication is that other areas will become off-limits if the behavior does not stop.

If you also ground the adolescent, you send an immediate message that he will be isolated from peer activities if he does not show better self-control. Most adolescents find time with their peers precious, so that actions you take in this area are likely to have some effect.

Your Younger Child Pokes Classmates in the Stomach and Taps Girls on the Behind

The child likes to play tricks on classmates and likes being the center of attention. The problem is that he is also violating their personal space, and his behavior has become physically abusive. Here it is important to work with the school to set firm limits but also to encourage the school not to suspend the child. Sending this child home is not likely to be seen as a negative consequence, except for you! Consequences like missing recess or gym or doing cleanup chores in the classroom after school are usually quite effective in stopping physically provocative behavior. Children generally do not like losing their free time.

Another important goal is to teach your child appropriate ways to get his classmates' attention. The child can be taught verbal ways to attract attention, like "hey can I show you this?" or "would you like to play this game?" When the child is trying to get your attention at home, show him appropriate ways to do this. Also, teach the child to deal with someone answering "no." When someone says "no," help your child to learn to ask someone else or to wait and do something himself for a little while.

You may also want to explain to your child that some of the other children may now be scared of him, and they may say "no" a lot because of his previous poking and tapping. Ask the teacher who he might pair off with, preferably someone who does not seem intimidated by him and who enjoys similar activities. Then consider having your child invite this potential friend to go somewhere fun on the weekend. One-on-one activities with a peer should be encouraged as a way to build relationships and social skills. Adult guidance may be needed to help your child not get too revved up while another child is playing at your house. If your child gets revved up with a peer present, you can suggest another calmer activity or actually engage the children in the activity for a little while before withdrawing into the background.

Your Child Talks Incessantly About How Well She Performed an Activity and Ignores Requests to Begin Homework

If you say firmly "stop talking about it and get down to work," your child may listen, or she may erupt into a rage because you have interfered with her narcissistic thoughts. An alternative strategy is to redirect the child by appealing to her narcissism. In order to do this, you need to tie the homework into her grandiosity. Find something about the homework that will appeal to her high opinion of herself. One example would be to make the homework into a contest. "I know you are an awesome pitcher, but I bet you cannot get this homework done well in the next half hour. If you give it your best, then we'll go see how awesome your pitching is outside." Here you have appealed to her competitive spirit, and in addition you have tied in the reward of watching her pitch afterward.

Another subtler way to appeal to her narcissism is to comment: "I want to watch how you can do this problem," or "I know you are good at this too. Show me what you can do." There are two elements here that connect to a grandiose child. One is telling her she is good at something, and the second is offering to watch her do it. Children usually enjoy the attention of having their parents watch them perform an activity, even homework. Grandiose children are especially gratified by having others watch and admire them. The key here is to watch with an admiring attitude. This is not the time to become critical of their homework.

If the child has begun her homework but talks at the same time about her prowess in another activity, it is recommended that you do not criticize her remarks. Let her talk about what she wants as long as she is also getting her work done. Remember the goal is to have the child complete her work, not to make her work quietly. If the child is in a group setting, and her talking is disturbing others, then it may be necessary to gently ask the child to talk a little more softly while others are working. "That's interesting," you could say, "but tell me a little more quietly while others are doing their work."

Your Adolescent Tells You He Is the Smartest Person in the Family and That Everyone Should Listen to His Advice

Your adolescent has a high opinion of himself. Why contradict him and precipitate a huge debate? Key into his actions not his words. In other words, it matters more what your adolescent does around the house than what he says.

You may worry that he could make the same kind of comments with peers and thereby alienate them. However, he may be saying this in part to get a rise from you, and he may know better than to make a similar remark in front of his peers. If you feel that your adolescent will say the same things in front of others outside the family and cause others to scorn him, then you can try some humorous, but not mocking, replies. "I wouldn't even listen to the president all the time." Hopefully, your adolescent will realize that no one listens to others all the time, not even him! Another implication is that no one knows everything, not even the president, not even your son. If your adolescent has a comeback, it is usually best to smile and enjoy his wit without getting into a contest of quips.

CHAPTER 4

ADHD and Depression

The Downward Spiral

Some ADHD children become lethargic, exhibit disinterest in school and friends, and feel hopeless. These are symptoms of depression. Researchers such as Biederman and Jensen estimate that between 13 and 30 percent of children and adolescents with ADHD also experience serious problems with depression. When these two disorders coexist, each exacerbates the other. For these children, their problems with attention in school lead to feelings of worthlessness. They feel like failures and often make up excuses to miss school. When these children do get seriously depressed, it makes it even more difficult for them to concentrate on school tasks, and their interest in other activities and in other people dwindles dramatically as well. When depressed, these children often do not want to take their ADHD medication, and, when they do, it does not seem to help.

Joseph: Disappointing His Parents

Joseph had shown symptoms of ADHD earlier but had not been diagnosed officially until presenting with depression, too, at nine years old. Joseph's parents reported that he was inattentive in school and usually forgot to bring home his assignments. He was also not well-liked by other kids in his grade because he did not know how to sustain friendships. There would be a disagreement with one friend, and then they became "enemies" in Joseph's eyes and he would stop playing with that friend altogether. Because Joseph was not particularly athletic and didn't dress like most kids his age, he was shunned and teased. He was also shy about asking anyone to play with him. Joseph explained, "No one likes me. Bobby bothers me. He said he'd hit me." When asked by a therapist about two boys he had played with occasionally in the past, Joseph replied, "I think David and Nelson do not like me. They say 'no' when I ask them to play. Every time I call a person . . . everywhere I go, people make fun of me." Notice how Joseph quickly generalized the rejection he felt from two of his peers. Joseph's negative thinking moved from a specific situation to a global sense of alienation, a hallmark of depression.

At home, his parents became increasingly concerned about Joseph's academic failures and met with his teacher and other school staff. They began a system in which both teacher and parents signed off in Joseph's homework book, so that Joseph's parents knew what the homework was, and so that the teacher knew that Joseph had shown the book to his parents. There were slip-ups, however, as Joseph did not write everything in the homework book, and the teacher did not always remember to let the parents know of all the assignments. In addition, Joseph sometimes misplaced completed assignments so that the teachers did not always get to see what he had worked on at home with his parents. When Joseph's parents finally heard about these problems from his teachers, they got extremely angry with Joseph, who cried and felt scared that his parents were going to hate him.

Joseph explained later in a family session, "I'm so afraid they are going to be disappointed in me." Mom added, "My husband harps on mistakes. He keeps going at it, and I can see Joseph shrink." Joseph then said with unusual insight, "I know [my dad's] bark is worse than his bite . . . he gets mad but then he calms down." Dad explained from his perspective: "I'm more disappointed if [Joseph] does not tell us. If he would only keep us informed when there is a problem, I would not get so mad." This was clearly a family with many unresolved issues. It took many months for the insights in this session to translate into changes in Joseph and his family's interaction at home.

In this case, Joseph's tearful reaction to the criticism by his parents was a clue to his coming depression. One might think that these blow-ups would help Joseph remember to bring everything home the next time. However, owing to the ADHD symptoms of inattention and disorganization, there was not a significant change in his follow-through with schoolwork—it was not something he could control on his own. As a result of the ADHD, there continued to be confrontations between the parents and the child, leading to tears and fears on Joseph's part. Because Joseph had no friends, there was no one to turn to when there were problems with his parents and teachers. His self-esteem eventually suffered, and he began to feel hopeless and worthless, wishing he were dead.

Betsy: When Adolescents Don't Outgrow the Problem

For adolescents with ADHD and depression, the failure to follow through on everyday life tasks may have serious academic consequences, such as failing classes or dropping out of school. High school and college-age children often do not let their parents, or others, help them, so that there is no safety net when assignments are not done or other problems arise.

The final years of high school were the beginning of some depressive problems for Betsy, who did not come for therapy until after she had started college. There were periodic fights with her parents about cleaning up her room. Piles of dirty clothes, papers, CDs, food containers, and the like were spread all over her bedroom, and the closet could not be opened without clothes falling out onto the floor as well. The parents were quite organized themselves and had tried over the years to devise strategies to improve Betsy's messiness. Occasionally there would be a major blow-up, and Betsy, in tears, would throw out some of the stuff and put the rest under her bed.

Betsy was also often late to school, and she sometimes missed school altogether because of stomachaches or headaches. But she was bright, and she still passed all her classes, often receiving better-than-average grades. Betsy took some pride in her ability to do a paper at the last minute and still get a good grade. Her procrastination made her parents anxious and angry.

Betsy was involved in after-school drama productions and made several friends there. She had fun after school and on weekends, and she showed no signs of depression when she was engaged with her friends. Although she had experimented with alcohol, there were no significant substance-abuse problems. Because of her good grades and interest in after-school activities, no thought was given to the possible therapeutic value of talk therapy or medication to address her issues. Betsy's cognitive and social skills helped her feel successful despite some early warning signs that her disorganization and mood were problems occasionally. The physical symptoms, Betsy's headaches and stomachaches, were the early signs that her emotional state was beginning to suffer. Lethargy in the mornings was another early marker of problems. But Betsy's parents were not too worried yet. They were told that many children have some of these problems and outgrow them. Though in hindsight we see that during high school Betsy had ADHD symptoms, such as disorganization and forgetfulness, as well as the beginning of some signs of depression, such as headaches and tiredness, she was still going to school and passing her classes. She had not come for evaluation or therapy yet.

Depression became a significant problem during Betsy's first year in college at a religiously affiliated school. She was unable to keep track of her school responsibilities when totally on her own, plus she felt no one really cared about her at school. Most of the other students in her school had a particular religious background that she did not share, so she did not bond well with the students in her dormitory. In addition, Betsy did not keep track of her finances and overspent on credit cards. Some of the companies began to harass her for payment.

Betsy explained how her depression came on in college: "I never learned how to pay my bills. I used credit cards and sent in payments when I had the money, which wasn't often. In my dorm, the other students prayed outside my door because they felt I worshipped false gods. . . . They also thought I needed prayers because I played role-playing computer games online. I didn't want people to know I was depressed, so I stopped going to classes and just stayed in my room." Betsy had stopped functioning: she wasn't going to meals, she was not bathing, and she did not talk with anyone. Eventually one of her dorm mates brought Betsy to the campus health services, and she was hospitalized for depression.

In general, interpersonal demands are greater when one is away from home for the first major period of time. The family provides a secure and organizing influence for the adolescent, like a safety net; without this net, some adolescents become disorganized to the point that they have trouble dealing with the social demands of living independently, not just the academic demands of a college. The key factors in Betsy's decline seemed to be her tremendous disorganization and her lack of significant social support. The disorganization extended beyond the academic to the financial and social areas of her life.

Ben: Needing to Break the Cycle

Another example of a child who had problems with mood and ADHD was Ben, age eleven. Like Joseph, Ben had problems with his peers and with his parents. Ben felt shunned by the other boys in school and in the neighborhood, who saw him as silly and not capable in sports—a double whammy that he was not athletic or socially skilled. His ADHD problems contributed to his social problems: he did not pay attention to social cues that others were tuning him out, and he did not wait until he had something interesting to say. Instead, he interrupted others with silly jokes and other out-of-place remarks. Another social liability was that he was a little overweight, and this became a source of teasing as well.

Ben's father often got very angry at his son's slowness in doing chores and his messiness around the house. When Ben did not accept his father's criticisms and did not immediately do what his father was asking, his father often exploded in anger. At this point, Ben would cry, and his mother would try to comfort him. The father would explain later in family therapy, "Ben gets me so mad. Why can't he listen to me? He has no respect for me. I'm sorry I called you names Ben, but you acted like such a baby." This insight came many months into therapy. Even then, Ben's father was still using words like "baby," which is humiliating to school-age children. During therapy, the father eventually learned to understand his son's forgetting to do chores as a common problem for boys this age, particularly children with ADHD.

In school, Ben frequently misplaced his work and had to do it over. His poor grades infuriated his father further because he felt his son was not trying. Not surprisingly, the father's anger did not lead to improvement in the son's performance in school. Rather, Ben's disorganization and inattentiveness in class continued. Something was needed to break the cycle of failure and Ben's increasing depressive mood.

Depression: What It Is, What It Isn't

We have been using the word "depression" to describe the moods of Ben, Betsy, and Joseph. What exactly is "depression"? Mental-health professionals often use the *Diagnostic and Statistical Manual of Mental Disorders (DSM-IV)* to help diagnose depression. The main criteria are sad or irritable mood and the loss of interest or pleasure in normal activities. The diagnostic manual uses the term "major depression" when either or both of these conditions are met for at least a two-week period. In addition, at least four of seven additional criteria must be met. These are changes in appetite (either increased or decreased), difficulty sleeping, changes in psychomotor activity (such that the person is either agitated or lethargic), feelings of fatigue, feelings of worthlessness, difficulty concentrating, and thoughts of dying. For "major depression" to be diagnosed, symptoms need to be present most days over a two-week period.

If, instead of daily problems for two or more weeks, there are *some* symptoms of depression present *on and off* over a year or longer, the diagnosis "dysthymic disorder" is used. For dysthymic disorder, not as many criteria need to be met, and they do not need to be met most days. However, dysthymic disorder, by definition, has to last at least a year for children and adolescents. It is, in a sense, a milder form of depression, but a longer-lasting one. It should be mentioned, though, that sometimes a "major depression" can last a year or longer, too.

If someone has some of these symptoms but for a shorter time, a diagnosis of major depression and of dysthymic disorder is not made. Many people have situational downturns that are reversed once the person has some time to heal. If a child is irritable or sad for a few days and then bounces back to a more normal mood, this is not called depression. This happens to some ADHD children when they do poorly in school, and it can be difficult to determine if their brief sadness or irritability is an early stage of a dysthymic disorder or depression, or if the problem is just a temporary setback. The child's mood would need to be monitored over several weeks or months to decide whether the child is becoming depressed.

Further, it is interesting that when problems persist and depression or dysthymia is diagnosed, the *DSM-IV* specifies that the young person's mood may be manifested as irritability rather than overt sadness. Many children do not appear sad and tearful when they are upset or depressed, but instead they get moody or crabby. This is in contrast to adults who suffer depression: adults usually appear melancholy and tearful. If a child's irritability persists, and if some of the other above criteria for depression are met, then the child would be considered depressed. For the purposes of this

73

chapter, a big distinction will not be made from here on between major depression and dysthymic disorder. They are like cousins, and the general term "depression" will refer to both.

Depression occurs when there are prolonged periods of sadness or irritability exhibited in more than one way in a child's life such as loss of appetite, sleep, energy, concentration, and interest in normal activities. The depression does not have to be exhibited in every way throughout the day, but it must last for more than a few days and it must affect more than one aspect of the child's behavior.

What if My ADHD Child Worries but Is Not Depressed?

Some ADHD children worry frequently about making mistakes in school or not being invited over by peers, but they do not show the apathy or low energy of a depressed child. These children do not show signs of depression; instead, their prominent symptoms are repeated worries about their performance and, sometimes, related physical symptoms, such as stomachaches. If the child has been in such distress for six months or more, the diagnosis would likely be generalized anxiety disorder (*DSM-IV*). Two scientists, Pliszka and Tannock, write that about 25 percent of ADHD children and adolescents suffer from some kind of anxiety disorder (generalized anxiety disorder, separation anxiety disorder, or phobias). For our purposes, we will focus on children who get frequent worries and sometimes physical symptoms like an upset stomach. This is called generalized anxiety disorder in *DSM-IV*. It is a symptom picture we sometimes see in ADHD children who have not developed a full-blown depression.

When a child has both ADHD and anxiety, it can be extremely distressing when he forgets something or receives a poor test grade—which, because of the ADHD will likely happen with greater frequency. He often berates himself, and he may agonize for hours or days about how he could have made so many mistakes.

Some anxious children may worry excessively that their overall grade will be low because of errors on a test. They lose the perspective that they may have been doing well on other assignments.

Bill, age eleven, had been diagnosed with ADHD and showed signs of anxiety about his inconsistent school performance but not depression. A bright child, Bill would at times forget the directions on an assignment and get everything wrong. Sometimes the teacher would let Bill do the assignment over, but sometimes she would give him a zero. When he received a poor grade, he worried about what was the matter with him. He would withdraw for the rest of the day in school, not speaking in class and keeping to himself on the playground. At home, his mother noted, "He worries for hours that there is something wrong with him and that he is going to fail fifth grade. It's hard to change the subject. He keeps asking, 'What's the matter with me?'" His overall performance in school was above average; in fact he received mostly As. However, Bill had difficulty keeping in mind his overall grades in school, and instead he chose to focus on that one single low grade.

Another problem for Bill was social interaction. No peers ever called him, and he wondered why. He was a shy child and did not want to call anyone himself. Bill reported anxiously, "I want to have a friend. Why doesn't anyone ever call? My sister gets called all the time." His worries were heightened when his sister had friends over to the house. When he was invited to a birthday party, his mother said that Bill worried about whether the child would like his gift and whether he would get teased at the party. Bill was not interested in sports, preferring to learn about bugs and animals. Eventually he became interested in a type of Japanese trading cards, which was an interest shared by some of the other boys at his school. This helped him connect at times with other boys his age, but Bill still was concerned whether the other children really liked him.

As we see with Bill, a particular difficulty for these dual-diagnosis children is forming friendships. They often do not enjoy social interactions because social interactions can be anxiety-provoking. Their brains are occupied by anxious thoughts, and they do not smile or interact comfortably with peers. In addition, their ADHD symptoms, such as distractibility, make them prone to social rejection as well. They may not pay attention to social cues and thereby suffer rejection. When these children do not get invited to parties or other social gatherings, their worries increase, which only makes it more difficult to relax and enjoy social interactions in the future.

An interesting cognitive problem for these dual-diagnosis children is what researchers have termed "working memory." Working memory has to do with keeping information in one's head in order to figure out the solution to a problem. When a person is writing, for example, the person must keep in mind the main purpose of the sentence, as well as make it flow from the preceding sentence and at the same time observe rules of grammar. Working memory is a kind of intermediate memory, as opposed to long-term memory. If one cannot remember all the data necessary to solve a problem, it will be difficult to successfully solve multistep math problems or write coherent essays, for example. Working memory is affected not only by the distractibility seen in ADHD children, but it is also interfered with by the anxious thoughts of children with coexisting anxiety disorders. If a child has a lot of anxious thoughts, the working memory becomes "full" with these thoughts, and there is little room left for thinking about the steps needed to solve an academic task. Thus, if a child has both anxiety and ADHD, it may be extremely difficult to do complex academic assignments. This problem is especially likely if the child is experiencing anxiety at the time she is doing an assignment, a situation that is quite common with these children.

Sometimes these children will develop depressive symptoms because they tend to be hyperaware of their repeated academic and social failures. Other children report numerous anxiety symptoms during childhood but do not get depressed. In both cases, self-esteem is often low, and periods of internal pain and self-doubt are likely. Many of the interventions we will discuss for the depressed child are also relevant for the ADHD child with anxiety. The strategies that have to do with building self-esteem are important for anxious children as well as for depressed children.

Interaction of Depression and ADHD

When a child has both depression and ADHD, each condition tends to aggravate and worsen the symptoms of the other. In the cases of Joseph, Betsy, and Ben, described earlier, the ADHD problems of poor organization and forgetfulness increased the child's and adolescent's failure experiences, which in turn contributed to the beginning of depression. In most cases, it seems the ADHD symptoms come first, and these are usually noted by the time the child begins school. Depression, on the other hand, often does not occur until later in childhood or adolescence. For depression to occur, there usually needs to be a series of events that negatively impact the person's self-esteem and lead the person "to give up" emotionally. For Joseph and Ben, it was the repeated blow-ups over homework that helped precipitate the depression. For the adolescent Betsy, it was the failure to do well in several areas of her life: academically, socially, and financially.

It is hard for parents not to react when their child keeps failing. The continued poor performance in school, as well as the repeated feelings of letting down one's parents, leads the child or adolescent to give up. Apathy becomes extreme. In addition, the child's level of self-criticism is usually extreme as well. It is not uncommon to hear a child say, "I hate myself." In our case examples, Joseph would make comments like, "I wish I were dead" when he experienced another conflict with his father over failing to complete his schoolwork. Some children will also blow up more frequently at others. The child may say "I hate you" at times of anger and despair.

Apathy and self-hate are symptoms of depression, and they are often pronounced in children with ADHD and depression. When ADHD is present, there are so many recurring problems with organization and forgetfulness that the child gets a regular dose of negative feedback from adults. As a result, apathy and self-criticism can become severe.

There is also a worsening of ADHD symptoms in these cases. Once the child or adolescent becomes depressed, the ADHD symptoms are often exacerbated. For many milder cases of ADHD, the children can tame their distractibility or impulsivity at times through internal effort or through external rewards and consequences. The child is motivated to try to pay attention, and this motivation helps somewhat. When the child becomes depressed, he loses whatever motivation he may have had. He tunes out even more. Thus, there is often a worsening of behaviors such as disorganization and forgetting where things are.

Why Do Only Some ADHD Children Develop Depression?

Not every ADHD child who experiences repeated failure develops depression. Researchers have shown that in addition to encountering repeated failures, ADHD children who develop depression often have a family history of mood or alcohol-related problems. There is a genetic predisposition to develop depression that is separate from the genetic basis for ADHD. One group of researchers discovered that family history for depressive disorders is not present in ADHD children who do not develop depression. Where there is a genetic predisposition and family history, depression is more likely to occur when a series of precipitating events occur, such as the repeated failures discussed in our three case examples.

Though there is a genetic predisposition to develop depression, we can lessen the likelihood for depression occurring by helping each child deal with negative experiences. Many studies have indicated that depression can be reduced and in some cases prevented by helping children change the way they view negative experiences. Martin Seligman writes that it is important for children to learn to take more responsibility for their successes and less responsibility for their failures. We will build on this idea in our treatment section to follow.

Another important factor that can inhibit depression is peer support. Many studies have shown that ADHD children who have trouble making and sustaining friendships—and as we've seen, this is a large percentage of ADHD children—are more at risk for developing depression. Having friends is protective of a child's ego in the face of the difficulties the child may have in school or at home.

We would expand this idea of the protective value of peer support to include any activity where the child consistently experiences success. We would call this area of success a "safety zone." A safety zone could be a sports or musical activity or it could be a social activity where the child feels important and valued. Or a safety zone could be a significant person in the child's life who continually boosts the child's ego despite the experiences of failure. Peer relationships are probably one of the most reliable sources of ego-boosting for children, but because of problems like distractibility and impulsivity, not every ADHD child develops a strong circle of friends. In that case, consistent adult support or a skill such as athletic aptitude would serve to protect the ADHD child from depression.

In the three case examples we discussed earlier in this chapter, there were no safety zones; in addition, in each case there was a family history of depression, indicating a genetic component. Recall that older adolescent Betsy had a safety zone in high school (her drama activities and her social activities on the weekends), but she lost these safety zones when she went away to college. The younger children Ben and Joseph did not have peer support, nor did they have an activity in which they excelled. There was no safety zone.

In summary, while most ADHD children are not prone to depression, about 20 percent will develop depression during their childhood. A family history of mood disorders and the absence of a safety zone, an area of success, are factors that increase the likelihood of depression. Once depression occurs in addition to

ADHD, symptoms like inattention, apathy, and self-criticism become accentuated.

Treatment for Depression in Combination with ADHD

Psychotherapy in conjunction with antidepressant medication has been shown to be helpful in treating depression. Unfortunately, there have not yet been treatment studies looking at the effectiveness of psychotherapy in dual-diagnosis cases. Some studies suggest that children with a dual diagnosis of ADHD and depression have a poorer prognosis than for either diagnosis alone. However, now that we are learning more about the characteristics of dual-diagnosis cases, we can plan more effective treatment strategies. The following section discusses strategies that are effective in outpatient treatment of dual-diagnosis children and adolescents.

For younger children as well as more severe adolescent cases, there needs to be a combination of individual and family treatment. The family is involved to help implement a behavior-modification strategy that aims to promote age-appropriate goals in school or in the workforce. For the younger child, the goals are turning in completed homework on time; for the older adolescent, the goals are regular class attendance as well as completion of major assignments, such as papers and tests. If the older adolescent has left school, the goal is to find and maintain a job.

Treating the Older Adolescent

The family and therapist work together to devise realistic expectations and meaningful rewards and consequences. For the older adolescent who has isolated himself during the early years of college, does not attend class, and often does not leave his room, the first goal is to attend class regularly. This might be rewarded by the parents paying tuition and allowing the adolescent unrestricted computer time in the evenings. The adolescent will probably need to live at home, because his parents could not employ a behavioral strategy if the adolescent lives outside the home and because the adolescent has no structure or safety net of peers to help him stay the course in school. After the goal of attendance is reached for one semester, minimal grades (Cs or higher) are expected the next semester. The student may still procrastinate, but he realizes his parents mean what they say and realizes they are trying to help.

It can be difficult using a behavior strategy with older adolescents because eighteen- and nineteen-year-olds have an age-appropriate need to be more independent of their parents. However, adolescents with dual diagnoses are too disorganized and too prone to exhibiting symptoms of depression if left without a safety net. Hopefully, in time, the adolescent will build a social network outside the home and require less supervision from the parents. In a sense, these children have a prolonged adolescence. There needs to be some respect given to these older teens in the way the behavioral plan is devised, however. Although the parents set certain limits, this is done with the adolescent's consent, and it is done in a minimal and realistic way. It would be too intrusive to set limits such as earlier bedtimes or forbidding altogether an activity that the adolescent liked.

In the case of the older adolescent, Betsy, a separate therapist was used for the family therapy than for Betsy's individual therapy. Betsy had shared personal information about her social life that she wanted to make sure would be separate from the family therapy, and the individual therapist did not want to take the chance that Betsy would be less open in individual therapy. In addition, in order to be effective, the family therapist needs to be allied with the parents as well as Betsy; the individual therapist felt Betsy was uncomfortable about "sharing" the individual therapist with the parents. Betsy said she was worried that the individual therapist might become less understanding of her point of view in the family conflicts if he met with her parents as well. So two therapists were involved in the case, and the family signed a release of information so that the therapists could keep in contact about the progress of therapy.

Betsy said to the individual therapist about the first couple of family sessions, "My mother harped on me about my room and about my bills. She thinks things are horrible. Bill collectors are calling me for money. She shouldn't listen on the phone. . . . And Dad printed fifty copies of a Christmas letter to all our relatives about my failures. I really got upset. Dad agreed to throw out the letters. Nothing I've done to improve means anything to them." The issue of privacy is a sensitive one for older adolescents. While you need to be involved in setting goals, it is generally unwise to listen in on your teen's phone calls without her permission. It is also unwise to tell all the relatives about your child's problems—this will only serve to humiliate her. Worse, your adolescent will then complain about the violations of her privacy and may miss the main point about working together on her disorganization. Notice that Betsy also lets us know how important it is for her parents to point out where she has improved. Though changes are usually gradual, it's important for you to praise your child regularly in order to promote the adolescent's emerging self-esteem.

In addition to family therapy, individual therapy for your older teen is a good idea. In these sessions, the therapist should first help your child to understand the dual nature of her diagnosis. Many times, teens don't recognize the way in which ADHD affects their organization and motivation for mundane tasks in and out of school; in fact, many think the problem only applies to their problems with paying attention in school. They are surprised and relieved to understand that their forgetfulness and difficulty managing the details of life, such as budgeting and paying bills in a timely way, are related to their ADHD. In addition, teens are often interested to learn how the ADHD impacts their mood and can contribute to depression. The therapist and teenager should review the teen's family history for mood disorders; this will enable your child to recognize the larger family problem and be less likely to blame herself for feeling depressed and unmotivated.

The therapist will also stress the importance of medication along with therapy, as it is often the case that the older adolescent has not been taking his medication regularly, believing that the medication would not be necessary if he only tried harder. Many adolescents, when fully understanding the nature of their problems, are more willing to take their medication every day.

Then comes the more difficult part of therapy, which is helping your child devise her own strategies and techniques for remembering mundane tasks in school and in life generally. In addition, once strategies are devised, it is critical to implement them on a regular basis, which is something that many teens have a problem doing. They are not really motivated to implement even the strategies they helped devise, because the strategies are fairly routine and require attention to details, something they still find uninteresting and difficult. An example of a strategy is to write appointments, or times to pay bills, on a calendar or personal digital assistant (PDA), and then remember to look at the PDA each day. Problems arise because your child often does not have the calendar or PDA with her, so that she either does not enter important dates or does not check back later. As a result, many times adolescents forget things, including appointments with their therapists!

A therapist skilled at working with ADHD youngsters who also have depression will have to have patience and empathy. Organizational issues need to be discussed regularly in therapy, but the therapist needs to be empathetic, remembering that these mundane details are sometimes more challenging for the adolescent than reading a novel or writing a paper. The therapist brings up in a noncritical way the price the adolescent pays for not attending to these matters. The therapist should not implement consequences or punish the adolescent himself, other than to point out real-life consequences and to help the family come up with a behavior-modification plan. There is a balance between understanding that the problems are caused by the teen's ADHD and depression, on the one hand, and helping the teenager stay aware of the consequences of her forgetfulness, on the other hand. Parents and therapists should try to maintain this balance. The aim in individual therapy is to help the teenager to keep thinking about her goals as well as the incentives and consequences, because it is attention to such details that the adolescent has trouble doing on her own.

In Betsy's case, follow-through with organizational issues was extremely difficult. She frequently overslept or forgot appointments, including those with the therapist. She was late handing in some important assignments for school and procrastinated about keeping her space at home in reasonable shape. The therapist would sometimes scratch his chin and wonder out loud, "How can you get on top of that? Your grades keep suffering when you turn in assignments late, and when you avoid picking up your stuff at home, it invites your mother to get on your case. How can you take charge of these issues?" The point of this intervention was to help Betsy see the price she pays for disorganization and to encourage her to think about ways she could handle things differently. The therapist uses phrases like "taking charge" because adolescents are interested in being in control of their lives.

In many sessions, we talked about her difficulty with carrying out her organizational goals, and we revised them in an effort to make them more fitting with Betsy's lifestyle (i.e., to do some chores late at night, or not to let herself go out on Saturday until the laundry was done). It was difficult for her to enforce her own rules. She did eventually carry around an appointment book, which helped her remember meetings and major school assignments. Her school performance improved, and she was late less often with schoolwork.

Betsy eventually graduated from college, and she and her family were quite proud of this milestone. She also caught up on her credit-card debts; her parents had taken control of her finances for about a year and gradually pulled back after that. Initially Betsy gave them the money from her part-time job, and they paid her bills. By the end of therapy, Betsy was paying her own bills and had gotten a debit card to use for purchases. We were all hopeful that she would keep track of her bank balance and not overuse the card. She was still living at home when we stopped therapy, and she continued to get into conflicts with her parents about her messiness. We were hopeful that she would soon be able to afford an apartment of her own.

Another goal of individual therapy is to help the adolescent develop a more positive view of herself and a more hopeful outlook about forming friendships. Part of this process is a review of the interpersonal problems she has had growing up. Many of these students have been teased or shunned because other children did not understand why they acted differently. The therapist explains that older peers are not so narrow-minded, and that differences in personality and behavior are more respected than when she was younger. Finding peers who have similar interests is a goal of the therapy process, but before the teen will work at developing new friendships, she has to develop some hope that these social efforts might be successful.

Another way the therapist helps this process along is by admiring your teen's strengths, which is something that all too often has been neglected in her life. This helps her develop self-confidence, which is necessary if she is to take chances in the social arena. In addition, role-playing is sometimes used to help your child practice the social skills that have withered or not been solidified along the path of life. During role-playing, the adolescent client pretends to be someone else, say a friend of hers, while the therapist pretends to be the client. The patient gets to hear how she sounds when the therapist talks as she would. Then the therapist discusses how the adolescent could change her approach, and finally they practice the new approach together.

All too often, the teen has subtly bought into the negative views others have had of her. For example, one young adult who had fared better in school than most still saw herself as a "goofball" in social situations. It was helpful for her to see how this view got started and to recognize her strengths, such as her beautiful smile and her special empathy for others. Her occasional giggling was reinterpreted as helping put others at ease rather than seen as a sign of "goofiness." It is important that the teen understand her differences from others—both the problems and the strengths. The teen is admired by the therapist for the struggles she has had to deal with in her life. With understanding comes self-appreciation and hope for the future.

Helping the Younger Child

For the younger child, more emphasis is put on family therapy than individual therapy; a major goal of family therapy is to have you, the parents, view your child realistically and more dispassionately. Often parents have grown so frustrated with the child's repeated forgetting that they blow up whenever the child forgets an assignment at school. They inadvertently contribute to the child's depression, rather than help solve it. The therapist helps the parents see that the process is an ongoing one—there will continue to be ups and downs.

One of the most important tasks for the parents and therapist is to *empathize* with the child who has ADHD and depression, keeping in mind that the child feels easily hurt and rejected. You, the parents, therefore, need to be patient and not expect too much too fast, and listen to the emotional undercurrent when your child is speaking. Especially at moments of terrible emotional pain, when the child feels like a failure, you and the therapist must show that you care. This is often difficult for frustrated parents to do.

Showing empathy and caring does not mean abandoning behavior-modification strategies, however, so the therapist will urge you to devise and stick with a behavioral plan. If the behavioral goal is remembering to bring home the books needed for homework, this means that we expect the child to remember more often—but not always. The key is to be realistic rather than aim for perfection. A therapist or the child's teacher can help you decide what realistic goals are and how much help to give the child to reach those goals. If you are too harsh in your criticisms, the child will avoid telling you about mistakes until they have multiplied and the teacher calls you to let you know of your child's difficulties. In fact, no matter how good parents' communication is with their child, there will be times children will avoid reporting mistakes or bad grades, as most young children fear any kind of parental disapproval and put it off as long as possible. Try not to lose your cool when this happens.

In the cases of Joseph and Ben, an important issue in the beginning of therapy was getting the parents to be realistic about their expectations and empathic with their sons' moods. Initially the therapist empathized with the parents' anger and pain about seeing their children have so many difficulties in school and at home—the parents were reacting naturally to a frustrating situation. In each case, though, we then devised a behavior plan to address the problems, and the parents were encouraged to be consistent with their plan and understanding of their child, rather than overly angry when the inevitable ups and downs arose.

In both cases, it was the fathers who were more impatient and angry with their sons' rates of progress. Ben's father had an especially difficult time becoming less emotional. "He acts like a baby. He doesn't do his homework and then cries when we get on his case. My father would have whipped my butt if I had acted like that. It gets to me when Ben doesn't listen to me. He's got to learn to respect me." This was Ben's father's constant refrain. Despite his son's diagnosis, he felt his son's disorganization and apathy were signs of disrespect. Several individual sessions were held with Ben's father to help him interpret his son's behavior differently and to stick to the behavior plan. What was also helpful in each case was the parents' trust in the therapist and their witnessing their child's pain in family sessions. Both fathers eventually realized that their sons weren't being lazy or disobedient, but they were really struggling to do better. They also saw that the behavior plan was working at least somewhat better than their previous strategy, which was to yell at their children.

It is also important for parents of younger children to help them find extracurricular programs for success and for social interaction with peers. Because many of these children feel unsuccessful and are shunned in school, it is critical to find an after-school activity where the child has some skill or interest. In a less academic environment, there is a better chance that the child will be recognized for his strengths rather than his weaknesses. If your child can develop a niche and receive admiration for it, then self-esteem will grow. The niche could be a sport like swimming or karate, a talent like reading or working on the computer, or even a hobby like collecting Pokémon cards. It is ideal if this niche is unique in the family, that is, not a skill that is shared by a sibling. The child with vulnerable self-esteem is probably already feeling less worthy than her siblings, so it is best to find a totally separate activity for her to excel in, if possible.

Social relationships are so important for children, and especially for children with these diagnoses. Relationships can help solidify self-esteem and provide the emotional safety net for children who tend to encounter more than their share of negative feedback in most classroom settings and might be prone to depression or anxiety disorder. In an after-school activity, the child has the opportunity to form peer relationships where he is less likely to be criticized by adults and less likely to be ridiculed by peers. Also, the activity becomes a common interest that the children can talk about together at other times. Through the activity, there is the beginning of a positive peer group, even if it is a small one.

In individual therapy with the preadolescent child, the main features of the dual diagnosis are explained in a way she can understand. Your child is told that remembering some tasks, such as homework, will be harder for her, but that she can do certain things to help herself out. The therapist talks about strategies, such as using one folder for homework and taking it with her throughout the school day. Other possible plans are discussed—perhaps letting you or your spouse go through the folder with her at night to help empty out unnecessary papers or having her teacher double-check the assignment book at school. It is also explained in individual therapy how important it is to be realistic about oneself, how sometimes she *will* forget and that people may get angry with her. Your child will be encouraged to let someone know when she is feeling really frustrated or upset. She'll first practice talking about her frustrations with her therapist. The therapist maintains a non-critical attitude and empathizes with her fears about how others will react. After your child is able to talk with the therapist comfortably about her painful feelings, she is encouraged to do so with you, her parents, as well.

In the cases of Joseph and Ben, they very openly shared their pain with the therapist *after* their parents had gotten angry about their disorganization in school. They talked about feeling like failures and cried about how their parents treated them. However, they did not talk with the therapist about failing a test or forgetting an assignment *before* it got to the point that their parents found out and punished them. It took several months before the boys were willing to share their disorganization problems on their own *before* they had gotten in trouble with their parents. The therapist encouraged the two boys to let him know when they were getting behind in their classes, but they tended to forget about it once they left the school building. The therapist explained that this is what they did with their parents and while this coping strategy helped them forget their problems and feel better initially, it led to pain later when their parents found out from their teachers about their poor performance.

Eventually the boys became more cognizant of their school performance before it reached the crisis level. In some situations, they shared the school problems with their parents after we had the parents promise not to be angry. It was interesting to see how the boys' initial coping style (of forgetting) and the parents' initial response (of rage) reinforced each other and made it difficult to break the cycle. Each time one of the boys forgot something and his parents found out, the parents got angry and the boys retreated further into their shell and became more and more reluctant to talk about what was going on. It took a fair amount of time for each boy and his parents to change their habitual way of responding to each other. Toward the end of therapy, Joseph came into an individual session and reported, "I lied again two days ago. When I got home from school, I said I had no homework, but I had a test to study for. I should have told my Mom right away. I ended up telling her, and she helped me study. No one screamed at me. I think I aced the test." This was a wonderful breakthrough for Joseph.

The child with ADHD and depression is often his own worst critic. He can put himself down as "stupid" when making a mistake even when his teachers and parents are understanding—and because his ADHD makes him more prone to certain types of "mistakes," the cycle can be very difficult. A therapist will help your child put the mistake in perspective. Your child will be taught some catchphrase like "everyone has bad times" or "so I make some mistakes, no big deal." These catchphrases help "normalize" mistakes and will help your child feel like everyone else.

Relaxation strategies, such as taking deep breaths, thinking about a favorite activity, or talking with the school social worker or guidance counselor, are all alternatives that your child is encouraged to pick from when she is upset at school. When your child is frustrated at home while doing her work, she should be encouraged "to take five" until she feels calmer. Unlike other ADHD children, those who are also self-critical need to "distract" themselves when they are upset. Most ADHD children may need to take breaks while doing a longer homework assignment, but the dual-diagnosis children may need extra "strategic" breaks when they feel upset.

Additional Techniques for Treating Anxiety Accompanying ADHD

As we've seen, there are many ADHD children who become frustrated and self-critical, but they do not develop a full-blown depressive disorder. Some children, like our earlier case example Bill, get anxious, but not depressed. For the anxious child, the above suggestions about raising self-esteem and changing harsh self-statements are crucial. The child with an anxiety disorder often has unrealistic expectations for success. Because he does not expect to make any mistakes, his worries and self-critical thoughts will be greater when he does at some point get a wrong answer. Parents and teachers want to model more benign thoughts, such as "everyone makes mistakes" or "with ADHD, you may make some mistakes, but you're a talented kid." Encourage the child to make these kinds of remarks to himself after getting back tests or homework papers. This does not mean, however, going to the opposite extreme of having no expectations for ADHD children with anxiety.

When your child with ADHD and anxiety worries about a weakness, encourage him to view his strengths, because having a more balanced viewpoint is helpful for lessening anxiety. Distraction is also sometimes useful: talking about a more benign subject while your child is in the throes of an anxiety attack helps to restore a child's sense of calm. Sometimes children refuse to be distracted, however, and will continue to obsess about their errors or failings. It takes time for children to feel more positive and less anxious. Biological interventions (which will be reviewed in Chapter 6) are sometimes helpful for children who hold on to their worries despite weeks of psychological interventions by parents and teachers.

Finally, if the anxiety builds to the point that your child does not want to go to school and develops panic symptoms, such as hyperventilating or nausea, it is important to have her go to school anyway. Do not talk a lot about school the night before; instead, use a distraction, such as television or games. When the child goes to school the next day despite her anxiety symptoms, she will more often than not see that the symptoms ease up after she has been in school for a little while. Her confidence about managing her symptoms will then increase in the days to come. If instead she were to stay home, her worries would dissipate for that day but return the next day with a vengeance, beginning a destructive cycle. Staying home is like rewarding the anxiety symptoms; so not surprisingly, they will increase in intensity in the following days.

Another approach for severe school anxiety is to use gradual desensitization: have your child go to school for part of the day, and gradually build up the time he stays in school over a week or two. In this way, your child's anxiety about school is broken into parts; he only has to face a couple of classes at first. Once he is more relaxed about attending these classes, it will not be so difficult for him to try a few more. By the end of a two-week period, he should be up to attending full days again. There may be occasional relapses when the child gets out of the routine of going to school following a vacation or a weekend. Sometimes there may be a rise in anxiety symptoms on the morning that there is a particularly difficult exam or project due. However, usually the desensitization does not need to begin all over again following a relapse if the child previously has progressed to going full days to school.

CHAPTER 5

Children with ADHD and Depression

Day-to-Day Problems and How to Deal with Them

Chapter 4 gave an overview of the diagnostic and treatment issues for children with the dual diagnosis of ADHD and depression. In this chapter, we will present a number of concrete situations that often occur with these children. Specific suggestions for parents will be given for each kind of problem behavior. There are three main groupings of problem behaviors for these children and adolescents: apathy and low energy, extreme disorganization, and self-criticism and self-isolation.

Apathy and Low Energy

You will need to work actively with your depressed ADHD child to reduce apathy and to increase energy. The key is working together on a plan with your child or adolescent. The child needs guidance from you, but he also needs to feel he is giving some input into what happens. Being involved in the plan will help reduce resistance from the child and increase his feeling of control over his own life.

One hallmark of depression is feelings of hopelessness and apathy. The opposite of these emotions is to feel active and involved in one's day-to-day life, so it is not surprising that the child's involvement in planning solutions with you helps to counteract his depression and apathy. However, because of your child's depressed mood, it is probably not easy to engage him in planning a resolution to day-to-day problems. Half the battle for you will be trying to engage your child in the behavior plan and helping him to see why he should even care about his life and what is going on. This will take time, patience, and listening skills on your part. Be persistent, but listen to your child's complaints at the same time. Try to find solutions that take account of your child's feelings. Be sure to stop and listen to your child's responses. Ask yourself: is my child participating in the discussion, or am I giving a speech while the child just sits quietly?

Here are some all-too-common scenarios in the homes of children with ADHD and depression.

Your College-Age Son Owes Thousands of Dollars on His Credit Card and Hasn't Made a Payment in Six Months

Your first reaction is one of anger at your son when a bill collector contacts you regarding this situation. How could he be so irresponsible? You also wonder if he has any money left in his bank account to pay bills. Rather than start screaming when your son wakes up, think about why this has happened and how you can help. The depressed adolescent with ADHD is often extremely disorganized and will find it quite difficult to keep to a budget. Once the bills accumulate, your adolescent may simply give up and ignore the bills. He may retreat into his room and feel hopeless to manage his financial affairs.

As the parent, you can help by talking about a realistic plan with your adolescent, a plan where you work together. Adolescents with depression and ADHD need structure and support to handle daily life tasks. One possibility is for your son to give you his credit cards, and for the two of you to think of how much money is available each month for bills and how much is available for spending on current needs. You could act as his banker: he gives you his paychecks, and you give him spending money each week. As the adolescent gets more motivated, gradually let him handle some of these tasks. For example, let him put his paycheck in the bank and withdraw the agreed-upon amount for weekly spending. You should go over the account with him when the monthly statements come in and determine together whether any changes are called for in the coming month.

The process of working with your older adolescent, however, is not usually as smooth as the above paragraph implies. He may resent your intrusion into his affairs, and, out of shame, he may deny that there is a problem. "They made a mistake. I'm not really behind in my payments," your son may say. In that case, be insistent that something be done, but, above all, be understanding. "Although keeping track of bills is not your strong suit, we love and respect you" should be your mantra. Mention some specific strength of his that you admire. A similar comment you could make that emphasizes working together is, "Okay, so paying bills is not your forte, but together we can get this worked out over time." If your son says that he does not want your help, insist. Let him know that you are still involved financially, as you are paying for his schooling or his room in your home, and, as a result, you still need to work together on financial matters. You can add that once he has a good job and can pay for everything himself, then he will no longer need your help.

It is possible that your son may storm out of the house or become withdrawn. Stay involved, and be empathic at the same time. For example, "I know this is hard for you, but you've got so many talents. I'm just acting as a secretary to help with mundane matters while you're still in charge of important life decisions. Once you have a regular job, you can hire your own secretary!" Suggest a plan of action and let him do as much as he can. You may not know how much he can do yet, until you try something out. It is trial and error until you come up with a plan together that works for your son and for you.

Your Child Looks Tired and Has No Energy for Starting Homework

Some children say they feel tired when they are asked to do homework or some other task they would like to avoid. You will need to think about whether your child is pretending to be exhausted or is exhibiting symptoms of apathy and lethargy, which are indicative of depression. One way to find out is to try an incentive or consequence that the child cares about. If the child is pretending to be tired, he will suddenly rally to avoid the consequence or earn the incentive. For example, offer an activity you know your child would enjoy, such as a trip to the park, when he finishes his homework. If your child is truly depressed, it is less likely that an incentive or consequence will matter. Depressed children tend to have little energy, particularly for tasks that are passive and routine, like homework.

When this lack of energy becomes a pattern, it is often very difficult for parents to help their child without feeling angry or drained themselves. However, there are activities and strategies that you can use to raise your child's physical and mental energy levels. You will also be able to (eventually) empower your child to use these strategies independently. Although initially these strategies may seem to require more of your own energy, in the long run, they will be less tiring for you to employ now than having to constantly nag your child to get going on his work. The keys to raising someone's energy are: choice of activity, mind-set, and informative feedback. Let us explain how you can choose activities to change your child's mind-set about homework.

Before your child begins her homework, think of a physical or mental activity that she likes. If she enjoys sports, you might try a brief sports activity such as shooting baskets, playing ping-pong, taking a short bike ride, or any other physical activity that can be done easily and quickly. Before beginning the activity, talk about how doing something physical actually gives us energy rather than using it up. Ask your child to rate her energy level before you begin. With young children, it helps to have them actually pick a number (say from one to ten) that represents their level of energy. As you and your child play or exercise together, find times to compliment your child on her efforts. When you are finished, ask your child to rate her energy level again, and tell her that you know this energy is going to carry over to her schoolwork. It's important to play long enough to enjoy the activity and feel energized, but not so long that you use up too much time and energy. Fifteen to twenty minutes is often a good amount of time, but you will need to experiment and see what works best for your child. Remember that *you* are the one setting a time limit for when the activity will end.

Many children find that they can raise the level of their mental energy by playing certain kinds of games or by working on puzzles that are quick but stimulating. You might choose games that are for two people, or you might choose puzzles that only the child will be doing. If you choose an activity that only the child will be doing, it is your job to act as a calm, but observant, cheerleader. Whichever you choose, it is important to label what is happening. For example, you can use a metaphor like, "Let's put our brains on high power" to help a child understand one of the goals for playing the game. Obviously the game or puzzle needs to be fun for the child, but she should also know that the game will give her the mental energy she needs to do her homework.

While the child is involved in the activity, be sure to compliment any behaviors that show good effort or even approximate good effort. Children love it when an adult says things like, "Wow, you solved that so quickly. I can see your brain is on high power." "You are using great thinking skills. This game is putting your brain on a strong thinking channel." "That was such a hard puzzle. I loved the way you kept trying new solutions until you got it right." Or "What great brain power you have!"

Once you do see your child's thinking getting on "high power," help her identify how this sense of cognitive energy feels. You might say something like, "Can you feel that your brain is on high power now?" or "What setting do you think your brain is on now?" Then tell your child that you know she can keep her brain on this setting while she does her homework. If your child feels ready to begin homework on her own, let her go ahead. Check on her occasionally, and compliment any efforts she makes to stay mentally engaged. If your child is unable to begin on her own, sit nearby and remind her that her brain is already on high power, so her homework is going to be easier than before.

Many games or puzzles can work to help a child develop a sense of mental energy, but certain kinds of games seem to work more quickly than others. There is a certain category of puzzles that provides a series of cards with progressively harder ways to set the puzzles up. The object of the puzzles is relatively simple, and the child can learn strategies by working her way through the series. Puzzles in this category include Rush Hour, Railroad Rush Hour, Safari Rush Hour, Lunar Lockout, Hoppers, and Brick by Brick. Some children can turn up their mental energy by playing simple card games that require memory skills, such as Concentration, in which the players have to remember which cards have been turned up and find pairs of matching cards. Other two-person games are also fine, but long board games, while fun, are not as successful in turning up brain energy. Recommended two-person games include things such as checkers, Chinese checkers, Quorridor, and Quarto (excellent for older students).

A note about video games: many children say that their brains go on "high power" when they play computer or video games; however, these games are rarely recommended as energy boosters. It is often very difficult for children to stop playing electronic games, and, further, children have difficulty labeling and transferring the energy they use with electronic games. When you are choosing your games, whether they are board or video games, ask yourself two questions: "Does this game encourage my child to think hard?" and "How long does this game normally take?"

Allow time for your child's past energy patterns to change. Even if you do everything "right" and can see that your child is able to work more easily when you use these strategies, it will take weeks of consistency to change the old patterns. Your child may also need "booster shots" of your interest and enthusiasm in order to maintain her energy.

Extreme Disorganization

It is important to plan together with your child when everyone in the family is calm. Organizational problems can infuriate parents, especially those who are fairly organized themselves. Wait until you have calmed down from witnessing a problem of extreme disorganization before beginning a discussion with your child. We discussed some examples of organizational problems in Chapter 1. When there is depression along with ADHD, these problems will likely be more difficult to treat, because the depressed child's energy level and motivation will be quite low. We made a number of suggestions for organization in Chapter 1 that will require extra patience and extra help from both teachers and parents when the ADHD child has depression. Because the teacher may not have the free time it takes to help your depressed child with organization, it will be helpful to your child if there is an aide at school to help him. For example, the aide could show your child how to organize his folders and backpack at the end of each day. As we encouraged before, begin slowly and take one organizational problem at a time. Be prepared to give more help in the beginning. Once the goal is achieved, everyone will feel some success, which will help propel you and your child to take on another problem together. For many children, especially younger ones, the parents will need to be quite active in structuring the situation by giving specific suggestions and reinforcing performance with incentives and consequences. While this process is time-consuming, it will help your child not only in the particular situation but also to develop a strategy that can be used throughout life to deal with organizational issues. Think about how long it takes for your child to learn to speak or to spell. Why should learning a life skill like organization not take a few years as well?

Your Adolescent's Personal Items Are in Disarray Throughout the House

The key here is to start with what bothers you the most. Set simple and clear standards. For example, food items in the family room may bother you more than shoes, papers, or a backpack left there. The rule then might be no food items outside the kitchen. Or the rule might be: if you eat in the family room, the plates or garbage must be removed immediately. Present this plan to your adolescent when everyone is calm. Discuss what bothers you, and ask how she feels. Explain that the new rule is important to you, even if it is not to her. There can also be clear incentives and consequences; for example, allowance money can be tied into the rule being followed. If you end up having to pick up food items, you can charge your daughter a fee each time you serve as her "maid." In the case of personal items such as clothes or toys being strewn about, the consequence can be that if you have to remove the items, they go in a bin until the end of the week, or until the adolescent does a task to earn them back. The most important thing for you to remember is that initially it will take some energy on your part to enforce the rule consistently. However, in the long run, your child will develop some new organizational habits. The child will see that she can organize some area of the house, and it is not as difficult or time-consuming as she may have thought originally.

This problem has to do with organization of space, whereas the next item on getting ready for school has to do with organization of time. Some ADHD children have problems in one area more than another; some have problems in both. When there is depression along with ADHD, children usually have many organizational problems. These problems may improve somewhat with psychotherapy and medication; however, structured approaches, like those we describe here and in Chapter 1, are generally needed to break the disorganization cycle.

Your Child Is Often Late to School or Work

Getting up for school in the mornings is especially difficult for the child with ADHD and depression. The child may take a long time to get out of bed and then daydream when he is supposed to be getting ready.

This is terribly frustrating to most parents, and there is often a lot of screaming in the morning while trying to get your child moving. Often he becomes distracted by some thought or activity that is not relevant to getting ready in the morning. It could be that he lies in bed, stands around in the bathroom, or sits in the kitchen or family room looking at television or at some toys. As parents, your first task is to figure out where things are breaking down and why. At what point does your child slow down or stop getting ready? Is the child daydreaming, doing another task, or enjoying some leisure activity, such as music or television? Is the problem because your child is disorganized without his medicine first thing in the morning, or does he not care about going to school or work? One contributing factor for many children with ADHD is that the medicine has not started working early in the day. Even when the child takes it in the morning, there is a thirty- to sixty-minute lag before the medication takes effect. Without the medicine, many ADHD children have trouble staying focused on mundane tasks in the mornings and thus need parental prodding. This situation becomes particularly problematic when your child is also depressed.

It could also be that the child does not care about going somewhere. Many depressed children are apathetic about many activities, in particular going to school. In that case, having natural incentives or consequences may help. For example, if an older child is not ready on time for school and misses the bus, charge a dollar or two "taxi" fee for you to drive him. For a younger child who is not ready on time, try reducing or eliminating some after-school privilege, such as time spent watching television. Another possibility is to build in a daily incentive for being ready: daily use of some family possession (car, computer, or telephone) could be contingent on getting to school or work on time. Each day would be a new day, so that the use of the family's possession on a given day would hinge on the specific task being accomplished first.

For parents who have to leave early for work themselves, it is especially important that your child develop time-management skills. You will not have time in the morning to micromanage your child. Sit down in the late afternoon or evening with your child when everyone is calm, and discuss how much time there is to get ready and what tools the child might use. For example, setting an alarm in the morning or having a watch that beeps at several intervals is often helpful. Maybe you can call home at a certain time to remind your child that it is time to leave the house. It is often trial and error to find a system that works for your child or adolescent. If something is not working, sit down again (and again) and discuss how to make it work. For children who are depressed and have ADHD, it often takes time to come up with a plan that works, because time management is an especially difficult problem for these children. It is important that you are not too punitive, as these children then might feel more like failures. For example, it would not generally be recommended to take away sports or after-school activities that are important to your child's self-esteem. Use a consequence that does not isolate the child from other people, and include incentives as well with depressed children, whenever possible.

If nothing is working, explain to your child how frustrating this is for you, and ask how it is for your child or adolescent. See if he will share some of his frustration with you. Sometimes suggesting the child talk (while the adult listens) helps the older child or adolescent to feel relieved and more ready to work out a plan.

Some older children or adolescents repeatedly blame you or others for their lateness. Try to set up the situation so that your child feels in charge. If you usually drive your child to school and end up nagging him when it is time to get into the car, a different approach would be for you to wait in the car a few minutes before it's time to pull out. Give a warning as you walk outside: "I'll be in the car." Now the older child is clearly in charge of getting out the door himself and cannot blame you for his lateness. Another possibility for older children is for you to wait some place in the house and for the child to call you when he is ready. Sometimes taking a step back and putting the older child in charge helps defuse a power struggle. By the way, the child may only care about being on time because he knows there are incentives or consequences that you have already set up together. Let the consequences you've set up do the job, instead of your constant reminders to get ready.

Self-Criticism and Self-Isolation

A major life task for all children is developing self-esteem and developing peer friendships. This is often a daunting task for children with depression and ADHD. Depressed children tend to be sensitive and easily hurt. They often interpret social happenings in a negative and self-critical way. For example, if a peer is busy and ignores him, the depressed child will immediately jump to the conclusion that the other child does not like him. In addition to depression, your child probably exhibits impulsivity, which is a hallmark of ADHD. Impulsive children sometimes blurt out inappropriate comments in social situations, which increases the chances that their peers will shun them. This, in turn, makes children with depression and ADHD feel even more vulnerable and even lonelier. Thus, the problem of ADHD with depression makes developing social confidence an especially difficult task.

Helping these children develop self-esteem and peer relationships can take years of patience and gentle encouragement by parents. The key is to try to empathize with your child's pain and then to help him develop a niche, or area, where he can successfully bond with peers. It is not important that he have ten or twenty friends, but rather one or two. Think about how many close friends we have as adults. Most of us were not the most popular people in school, nor are we about to run for mayor of our hometowns! However, it helps to have one or two people share life's joys and sorrows.

Your Child Says He Is the Worst Baseball Player on His Team and Wants to Quit

First think about when the child said this and what was going on. Did something particular happen on the ball field that day, or did a peer say something at school? Ask the child what makes him think so. If he does not have an answer, ask a more general question, such as what happened today? If the child mentions being teased or being struck out, one approach would be to reframe the child's interpretation of these events. For example, if the child struck out, explain that everyone strikes out, even star players. In other words, striking out does not make you a lousy ball player. Maybe there was a good pitcher today, or maybe your child had an off day. Help your child interpret the event in a more benign way. Often depressed children believe they are the cause of their problems rather than being able to look at alternatives.

If your child truly lacks skill in baseball, think about why. Does he get distracted in the field while waiting for some action? Does he have difficulty with eye-hand coordination? Be realistic about your child's abilities, and try to find a niche that works for him. Rather than baseball, would a sport like swimming work better, because there is less emphasis on eye-hand coordination and also less emphasis on waiting and watching? Or does your child have another interest or talent other than sports? It is important for your child's self-esteem that he finds a niche where he is comfortable.

If your child is in the habit of making disparaging remarks about himself in order to get your attention, it may be wise to ignore some of them. Say nothing or talk about something else. Sometimes this approach works to help the child switch to another thought and mood and puts an end to particularly negative self-statements.

Your Adolescent Regularly Stays in All Weekend and Does Not Call Anyone

Your adolescent may feel no one likes her or will want to see her. Ask what she thinks is wrong. If she really prefers to be alone, do not be too pushy, or she will feel she is disappointing you and that could lead to more depression. It may also be the case that your child or adolescent has felt rejected so often that she has given up. In that case, be empathic and listen to her pain. In time, try to guide her toward a weekend activity for which she has some interest and/or aptitude.

If she wishes she had a friend, help her think of a classmate she can call or an activity she can join where she could meet others. The activity should be one she enjoys and one where she could meet other young people without having to call someone on the phone. Initiating a get-together through a phone call can be difficult for many shy or depressed children. If she would consider calling someone, role-play the situation ahead of time. Another possibility would be for you to offer to invite the family over, which would be a way for your adolescent to have a friend come over without having to make the first move. Your support may help get the process started. If not, think about talking to the school counselor about ways to build social skills or social confidence through a school activity.

If you and your child are not successful finding a social activity for her, then in the meantime you should plan some family outings. You will be her "friend" for the day: you could go to the movies or shopping together, or you could go watch a sport the two of you enjoy. The goals here would be to help your child get more active and to see how she handles the outing. Your child will probably enjoy the outings with you and, in time, may be motivated to do similar activities with other people when you are busy. If part of the problem is low energy, then doing things together will help lift her mood.

If you determine that your child has limited social skills during the outing, then you may work on this with her or ask the school counselor to do the same. For example, you may find that your child does not answer your questions or ignores you. Point this out to your child or adolescent, and tell her gently how it feels when you are ignored. Another possibility is that your child may talk with you but not really be attuned to your feelings. You may be tired or bored at some point, and your child may not pick up on it. You could stop what you are both doing for a minute, and explain how you are feeling. Show your child how she can tell in the future that you are bored. Later that day, or on another outing when the issue comes up again, see if she can pick up on the problem, or else stop what you are doing and help her again to figure it out. You may need to do this a number of times before your child gets sensitized to the signs that you are bored and develops a verbal strategy to deal with it. For example, you could teach her to suggest that you either should rest or get a bite to eat, if either of you feels tired or bored. The first step is to teach your child to recognize signs that someone is bored, and the second step is to teach her what to say then.

CHAPTER 6

Medications for ADHD and Mood Disorders

The role of medications in the treatment for ADHD and mood disorders in children and adolescents is an emerging area of pediatric psychiatry. At present, there are few large-scale medication studies of ADHD children with additional diagnoses. A 2004 study was carried out in Texas that developed treatment algorithms (a suggested order of medications) for various diagnoses including the combination of ADHD with depression. The study's recommendations are included in our later suggestions for treating children who have both ADHD and depression.

There have been more studies of mood disorders alone, without ADHD. Most of the research to date on mood disorders is with adults, which generally shows that medication alone or medication combined with psychotherapy is effective. In 2004, researchers at Duke University, in cooperation with the National Institute of Health, investigated the treatment of depression in adolescents. They found that medication combined with cognitive-behavioral therapy is superior to medication or psychotherapy alone. Although somewhat less effective alone, each form of therapy was also helpful in its own right for treating depressed adolescents. There are few large-scale medication studies of mood disorders in preadolescent children, although there have been a number of small studies. While we wait for more research, clinicians are developing strategies for treating children who have ADHD and mood disorders. Medication plays an important role in treatment, because both ADHD and mood disorders have biological components. The question becomes which disorder do you treat first? Other questions parents often have are what are the side effects, and are there possible drug interactions if you later add medications for the second problem? First we will consider the diagnosis of ADHD with depression, and then we will review what to do for ADHD and bipolar illness.

ADHD and Depression: Where Do You Start?

Betsy, the adolescent we introduced in Chapter 4, suffered such severe depression in college that she was started on antidepressants in the hospital. The antidepressants were necessary because Betsy was not taking care of her own basic needs, had not left her dorm room for days, and expressed suicidal thoughts. In fact, the doctors were so concerned about Betsy's depression at that time that they did not evaluate her for other problems, like ADHD. At the time, she was treated only for depression. With therapy and antidepressants, her mood improved, and she returned home.

Several months later she began outpatient therapy. She signed up for classes at a local college, but she was having a lot of difficulty concentrating and doing assignments. Betsy's history indicated that she had a long-term difficulty with attention in school. In addition, there were signs of disorganization in many areas of her life. Thus, she was finally diagnosed with ADHD along with depression. In fact, the history showed that her attentional problems had existed since elementary school days, while her depression did not start until college. ADHD medications were added to her antidepressants. The combination of medications helped her much more than the antidepressants alone. Her concentration in classes improved. However, it took a lot of work in psychotherapy to help her stay focused on long-term goals and to help her with disorganization problems.

Many important principles about medication for ADHD and depression are illustrated in Betsy's case. First, medications alone do not usually solve the problems. Family and individual therapy were needed in addition to medications in order to help Betsy overcome her longstanding difficulties in organization and apathy about her responsibilities, like paying bills on time. Medications were helpful in improving Betsy's energy level and concentration, but Betsy also needed to learn new skills to manage her academic and financial affairs. This is where therapy was helpful. In therapy, Betsy learned why she was avoiding day-to-day tasks, and, more importantly, she learned skills to manage her affairs. She realized that the costs of not doing so had severely affected her academic, financial, and family life.

Another important principle that this case illustrates is that a combination of medications to treat both ADHD and depression is better than treating just one disorder or the other. A 2004 study called the Texas Children's Medication Algorithm Project is one of the first to look at the use of medications for children with ADHD and depression, and it confirms that a combination of medications is often needed.

One more principle about the treatment of ADHD and depression is illustrated by Betsy's case: the most critical problem is treated first. When Betsy was hospitalized, her depression was severe, and this was the primary focus of medication and psychotherapy. What is atypical in Betsy's case is that there was such an extreme level of one problem relative to the other; in other words, her depression was quite severe in relation to the more moderate level of her ADHD. It is more common to find a moderate degree of both attention and depression problems when children first appear for an evaluation. However, it isn't surprising that Betsy's ADHD was diagnosed relatively late in life: her intellectual abilities had helped her cope in high school and delayed an evaluation until her depression became severe.

When Both Problems Are of Similar Intensity

For the two child cases we introduced earlier in Chapter 4, there were moderate levels of depression and ADHD in both boys. Joseph was having difficulty keeping track of and completing his homework. When he received zeros for failing to complete assignments, his parents became enraged, and Joseph would cry and feel like a failure. His mood was negative at these times, but he was still able to get out of bed and attend school regularly. He was apathetic about school but not totally isolated and withdrawn, as Betsy had become at one point. Ben, our other case study of depression and ADHD, was also able to participate in school and family activities. There was some apathy about school and peers, but not extreme withdrawal from life activities.

In these two cases, it was decided to treat both disorders at about the same time. However, in order to be sure that we know which medication is having what effect, we generally try one medication first for several weeks, followed by the other medication. With children such as Ben and Joseph, we start with the ADHD medications, either atomoxetine or one of the stimulants: methylphenidate, dextroamphetamine, or dextroamphetamine combined with racemic amphetamine. (Table 1.1 shows the appropriate dosage range for ADHD medications.) There are three reasons why we usually start with one of the ADHD medicines. First, if recognized early, the depressive symptoms are usually rather mild. Second, most ADHD medications are short-acting, so that the doctor, parents, and teachers can often get an idea in a few days if the medication is helping with attention and hyperactive behaviors. Third, we want to find out whether there might be a recovery in mood once the ADHD symptoms are treated. In a few cases, a child's mood recovers within two to three weeks of ADHD treatment, and the mood disorder goes away on its own accord. If the child's attention improves dramatically, and if he receives positive feedback from teachers and parents, his mood sometimes improves significantly.

Often the child's mood is unchanged, and the antidepressants are added. As we've seen in most cases, there is a genetic predisposition to develop a mood disorder, so the child's ADHD is not the only thing "getting them down." In addition, there has usually been negative feedback from adults for a long time owing to the child's poor attention and disorganization. A week or two of positive feedback will not undo years of the child feeling like a failure. Furthermore, there usually continue to be symptoms of ADHD, even when ADHD medications have been helpful. There is some improvement in attention, but most children still have difficulty with organization and impulsivity. Thus, the child will likely continue to experience difficulties succeeding academically and socially, which may contribute to the mood disorders. As a result, additional treatment of mood issues is often necessary.

Antidepressant Medication

Before adding an antidepressant to your child's ADHD medication, a psychiatrist will assess the degree of depression, its course, and the response to interventions so far. The clinician usually will involve the patient and family in the decision process and provide education about the medication and its effect on depression and ADHD.

Assuming the symptoms of depression are persistent despite treatment of ADHD, then a trial of antidepressants often is begun. The effect of antidepressants often is gradual so that it will take one or two months to evaluate whether the medication is effective. Selective serotonin reuptake inhibitors (SSRIs) are the initial medication choice for children and adolescents. Essentially, these medicines allow serotonin, an important neurotransmitter (chemical) in the brain, to be used more effectively. Here is how we think the SSRIs help: there is an inefficient use of serotonin when a "sending" nerve cell in the brain retrieves serotonin and breaks it down before the serotonin can attach and communicate with a "receiving" cell. The SSRIs prevent serotonin from being prematurely retrieved from the space between the sending and receiving cells. As a result, serotonin will be available longer at the "receiving" nerve cell in the brain. The availability of serotonin

TABLE 6.1 Comparison of SSRI Antidepressants

Brand Name	Celexa	Lexapro	Zoloft
Generic Name	Citalopram	Escitalopram	Sertraline
Initial Dosage	20 mg	10 mg	50 mg
Maximum Dosage	60 mg	20 mg	150 mg
How Supplied	Tablets: 20, 40 mg; oral solution: 10 mg/5 ml	Tablets: 20, 40 mg; oral solution: 1 mg/ml	Tablets: 25, 50, 100 mg; oral concentration: 20 mg/ml
Time to Response	4–6 weeks	1–2 weeks	4–6 weeks
Half-Life	32 hours	27–35 hours	26 hours
Mechanism of Action	Selective serotonin reuptake inhibition	Selective serotonin reuptake inhibition	Selective serotonin reuptake inhibition
Adverse Events (from Adult Studies) >10%	Dry mouth: 20% Sweating: 11% Nausea: 21% Somnolence: 18%	Nausea: 15%	Insomnia: 16% Nausea: 26% Diarrhea: 18% Somnolence: 13%
Cytochrome P450 Isozyme Inhibition	Mild	None	Significant
Psychiatric Medications Not to Be Used at the Same Time as the Above Antidepressants	MAOI	MAOI	MAOI

is what we believe leads to an improvement in depressive symptoms so that the person can deal better with life events.

Recent clinical trials with children and adolescents who have only depression have shown the effectiveness of a couple of SSRIs, namely fluoxetine (Prozac) and paroxetine (Paxil). Studies of dual-diagnosis children are ongoing. Clinical trials of many other antidepressants have been performed in children, but the findings were inconclusive or negative, even though adult studies have supported their effectiveness in treating depression.

Table 6.1 lists commonly used antidepressants for children and adults. All of the medications listed became available in the past two decades and have few side effects. Only fluoxetine (Prozac) has been approved by the FDA for the treatment of depression in

Paxil	Paxil CR	Luvox	Prozac
Paroxetine	Paroxetine	Fluvoxamine	Fluoxetine
20 mg	20 mg	50 mg	20 mg
60 mg	60 mg	300 mg	60 mg
Tablets: 10, 20, 30, 40 mg; oral suspension: 10 mg/5 ml	Sustained release tablets: 12.5, 25, 37.5 mg	Tablets: 25, 50, 100 mg	Capsules: 10, 20, 40 mg; oral solution: 20 mg/5 ml
4–6 weeks	4–6 weeks	4–6 weeks	4–6 weeks
21 hours	21 hours	15 hours	96–384 hours
Selective serotonin reuptake inhibition	Selective serotonin reuptake inhibition	Selective serotonin reuptake inhibition	Selective serotonin reuptake inhibition
Nausea: 26% Somnolence: 23% Insomnia: 13% Asthenia: 15%	Dry mouth: 15% Nausea: 22% Diarrhea: 18% Somnolence: 22% Insomnia: 17% Dizziness: 14% Constipation: 10%	Nausea: 36% Insomnia: 32% Agitation: 32% Headache: 22% Somnolence: 27% Asthenia: 29% Dizziness: 15% Anorexia: 15%	Dry mouth: 10% Tremor: 10% Nausea: 21% Somnolence: 13% Insomnia: 16% Anxiety: 12% Anorexia: 11% Nervousness: 14%
Significant	Significant	Significant	Significant
MAOI, Thioridazine	MAOI, Thioridazine	MAOI, Thioridazine	MAOI

children and adolescents. However, the medications that have been approved for use in adults are also used in children.

While antidepressants are often helpful in treating depression in children and adolescents, the FDA issued a warning in late 2004 that these medicines may increase suicidal thoughts or actions in some children and teens. Researchers looked at youngsters who took either sugar pills or antidepressants for one to four months. Although no one committed suicide in these studies, some young patients became suicidal. On sugar pills, two out of one hundred became suicidal. On the antidepressants, four out of one hundred youngsters became suicidal. The FDA recommended that parents and doctors pay especially close attention to possible suicidal thinking during the first four weeks when a child or teen begins an antidepressant and also whenever the dose is changed. Weekly meetings with the prescribing doctor are recommended when the medication is started or the dosage altered. The time between appointments is then gradually increased. If parents see a worsening in depression, anger, hyperactivity, anxiety, or irritability, the FDA recommended that the child's doctor be notified. The risk of suicidal thinking becoming worse in these cases is low. However, it is important to be cautious in order to make sure the child is safe.

The majority of the antidepressant medications require two to six weeks before depressive symptoms begin to improve as indicated in Table 6.1 under "Time to Response." In clinical studies thus far, only escitalopram (Lexapro) has been shown to require just two weeks for a significant improvement in depressive symptoms. The remainder of the antidepressants usually require approximately four weeks for a significant resolution of depressive symptoms.

Table 6.1 lists approximate doses for SSRIs in the pediatric population. The dose should be increased gradually over one to two weeks to an initial target dose. If the dose is increased too rapidly, there is a higher risk of adverse events. Once the initial target dose is reached, it should be maintained for four to six weeks unless the patient's symptoms worsen or adverse events occur. If depressive symptoms persist after four to six weeks, then the dose may be gradually increased over two to four weeks in order to improve symptoms. Sufficient time should be allowed in order to determine the efficacy of the new dose before increasing the dose again.

Failure to respond to an initial SSRI should be followed by a trial of an alternative SSRI, which in turn should be followed by an alternative class of antidepressants. The SSRIs focus on the brain chemical serotonin, whereas the alternative antidepressants increase various other brain chemicals that can affect people's depressive symptoms. Examples of the alternative class of antidepressants, shown in Table 6.2, are venlafaxine (Effexor XR), duloxetine (Cymbalta), and bupropion (Wellbutrin XL). Prior to making changes, however, it is important to reassess the initial

TABLE 6.2 Atypical Antidepressants

Brand Name	Wellbutrin XL	Effexor XR	Cymbalta
Generic Name	Bupropion	Venlafaxine	Duloxetine
Initial Dosage	150 mg	75 mg	40 mg
Maximum Dosage	450 mg	225 mg	60 mg
How Supplied	Extended release tablets: 150, 300 mg	Extended release capsules: 37.5, 75, 150 mg	Capsules: 20, 30, 60 mg
Time to Response	4–6 weeks	4–6 weeks	4–6 weeks
Half-Life	21 hours	13 hours	12 hours
Mechanism of Action	Dopamine reuptake inhibition	Serotonin and norepinephrine reuptake inhibition	Serotonin and norepinephrine reuptake inhibition
Adverse Events >10%	Dry mouth: 17% Headache: 26% Nausea: 13% Constipation: 10% Insomnia: 11%	Dry mouth: 12% Sweating: 14% Nausea: 31% Somnolence: 17% Insomnia: 17% Dizziness: 20% Nervousness: 10%	Dry mouth: 15% Nausea: 20% Insomnia: 11%
Cytochrome P450 Isozyme Inhibition	Significant	None	Significant
Psychiatric Medications Not to Be Used at the Same Time as the Above Antidepressants	MAOI	MAOI	MAOI

diagnosis and evaluate whether there are other factors impeding treatment. For example, is the child or adolescent refusing to take the medication some days? Failure to take the medication on a regular basis can prevent its effectiveness. Are there significant problems in the family or school that are bothering the child on a daily basis? Continual negative feedback at home or school can impede the effectiveness of antidepressants. Is the adolescent patient abusing alcohol or substances of some kind that can interfere with the antidepressant? All these factors need to be discussed with the patient and family. Consultation with the child's therapist may also help rule out some of these factors.

Most side effects to SSRI antidepressants are not severe and usually resolve themselves within a few days. Side effects seen in

SSRIs and other antidepressants include insomnia, headache, dizziness, nausea, and "behavioral activation." By "behavioral activation," we mean increased energy and activity, beyond what is normally shown by that child. These side effects may occur any-time, but more likely within the initial week of medication, or when the dose is increased. They occur in 10 to 20 percent of cases and usually subside within a week. It's important to note that one symptom, insomnia, may be a side effect of SSRIs, but also may be a symptom of depression. It usually improves with con-tinued treatment with the SSRI, but sometimes the medication will need to be discontinued, or another medication added for sleep. Another side effect in 3 to 6 percent of cases is manic-like behavior. Mania symptoms usually subside quickly with the dis-continuation of the antidepressant. And, as we've noted above, the alarming side effects of suicidal thinking and behavior are rare, but need to be assessed at the outset of treatment, and whenever the dose is raised or lowered.

Drug interactions are important to consider when taking more than one medication. With psychiatric medications, however, drug interactions are particularly common and can have undesirable effects. Some antidepressants can interact with other medications, including some ADHD medications, through their effects on liver metabolism. Tables 6.1 and 6.2 indicate those antidepressants that affect the liver's cytochrome P450 isoenzyme system. When taking two or more medications that interact with this system in the liver, it is imperative that a psychiatrist who is knowledgeable of the potential drug interactions closely monitor the medications and respective doses. For example, fluoxetine (Prozac), paroxetine (Paxil), sertraline (Zoloft), and duloxetine (Cymbalta) inhibit the P450 isoenzyme 2D6, which is involved in the metabolism of many other psychiatric medications. This interaction is very important because any medication that is given with fluoxetine, paroxetine, sertraline, or duloxetine may need to be at a much lower than usual dose. Otherwise there can be a range of problems from toxicity to decreased effectiveness of the other medications. Of the common ADHD medications, atomoxetine is metabolized the most by the cytochrome P450 2D6 enzyme. When this ADHD medication is given along with one of the antidepressants listed, then the dose of one or the other will need to be lower than usual. The dose of amphetamine, either Adderall or Dexedrine, if given with one of the SSRIs, may need to be adjusted as well, because preclinical studies not involving humans indicate some metabolism of amphetamine by the P450 enzyme system.

When ADHD medications are given concurrently with antidepressants, special attention must also be given to the dosages if both medications can increase the amount of available neurotransmitters (like serotonin or norepinephrine) in the brain. Specifically, too much serotonin can cause side effects like dizziness or shivering or, in rare cases, hallucinations, seizures, or blood-pressure fluctuations. The amphetamine (Adderall) and some antidepressants, namely the SSRIs and duloxetine, increase the level of serotonin, so that one or the other may need to be lowered when they are used in combination. Another ADHD medication, atomoxetine (Strattera), increases the amount of norepinephrine available in the brain, as do the three atypical antidepressants listed in Table 6.2. Thus, the dosage of one of these medications may need to be lowered when given in combination.

How long should children and adolescents continue to take antidepressants? There is no research evidence yet about the incidence of relapse in children and adolescents. Therefore, the guideline for how long to treat an episode of depression in children and adolescents following remission is the same as adults, approximately four to six months. Presently, it is not possible to determine which patients require prolonged treatment to prevent new episodes of depression. Generally, patients with severe depression or a history of previous episodes are likely to be treated for a longer time than six months. Sometimes in these patients, after a period of a year, the medication can be gradually discontinued without a relapse; however, sometimes antidepressant medication may be needed for years.

When stopping antidepressant medication, the dose should be decreased gradually in order to avoid side effects. Possible side effects include headache, agitation, restlessness, fatigue, and depression. These discontinuation side effects are especially common for paroxetine owing to its quick biologic elimination. Other commonly used antidepressant medications that have relatively quick biologic elimination and thus necessitate gradual tapering downward include bupropion, duloxetine, fluvoxamine, sertraline, and venlafaxine. As mentioned earlier, there is also a very small risk of suicidal thinking or behavior whenever the dose of antidepressants is changed, and this would include the discontinuation phase of treatment.

Children will usually need to continue with their ADHD medication for a long time. Treatment of ADHD is usually necessary for years, at least while the child is in school. Many older adolescents and adults also benefit from ADHD medicine, particularly when they have difficulty with tasks requiring sustained attention and reflection. If the ADHD symptoms are controlled, there is less likelihood for recurrence of depression.

Medical Treatment of Dysthymia and ADHD

In Chapter 4 we explained that dysthymia is a milder depression that occurs on and off over a year or more. While clinical research has shown that antidepressant medications and psychotherapy are effective in the treatment of major depression, the optimal treatment for dysthymia has yet to be determined by clinical research. How does one treat dysthymia and ADHD then? In most cases it is appropriate to first treat the ADHD with the medications that are indicated for ADHD—that is, the stimulants or atomoxetine. Sometimes the dysthymia will resolve with successful treatment of the ADHD. However, psychotherapy and antidepressant medication, such as the SSRIs, often are needed to help resolve the depressive symptoms of dysthymia. A sometimes practiced, off-label approach to treating both dysthymia and ADHD is the antidepressant medication bupropion (Wellbutrin SR; Wellbutrin XL). Bupropion XL (a longer-acting version) is taken in the morning, or bupropion SR (a shorter-acting version) is taken in the morning and late afternoon, for the treatment of depression. In some instances, bupropion successfully treats both the dysthymia and ADHD without the use of an additional ADHD medication. However, ADHD medications are usually needed for the optimal treatment of ADHD symptoms.

Medications for Treating Anxiety and ADHD

If the child has not developed depression, but shows signs of anxiety along with ADHD, then the first line of treatment is one of the ADHD medications combined with psychotherapy. We treat the ADHD symptoms first because we want to see if there is any improvement in anxiety before considering whether to add an antianxiety medication. If anxiety symptoms are not improved, we would try adding one of the SSRIs, as these generally help anxiety or depression. If they are not effective, a small dose of an antianxiety agent, such as buspirone, could be tried. This medication has been approved for treatment of anxiety disorder in adults, but not for children. Buspirone does not have addictive qualities. In contrast to buspirone, some antianxiety agents such as alprazolam and clonazepam have potential addictive properties if used long term, so that they should be discontinued within several weeks.

ADHD and Bipolar Disorder: Treating the Highs and Lows

Alan was the teenager we wrote about in Chapter 2; he had such extreme mood swings in a single day that it was very difficult for his parents to manage his outbursts. One minute he would be on a "high" and would talk about how much he and his girlfriend loved each other, and the next minute he could be in a rage if his parents told him he could not see her one evening. His mood also occasionally shifted to extreme depression whenever his girlfriend did not want to see him. During periods of rejection, Alan expressed suicidal thoughts and at times made superficial cuts on his arms with a razor. Usually within a week or two, he would find a new girlfriend and become excited again. While a romantic relationship was ongoing, his mood rarely got depressed.

When Alan came for psychotherapy, he had already been treated with stimulant medication for ADHD. It had no effect on Alan's mood swings and had only a small impact on his distractibility in school. When a child is on a "high," he will continue to have problems with distractibility and impulsivity despite treatment with ADHD medication. Bipolar illness contributes to problems with distractibility and impulsivity, and bipolar illness does not respond to ADHD medication.

The psychiatrist in this case saw Alan during a depressive episode and decided to add an SSRI antidepressant. After four weeks at the target dose, the mood swings worsened, and there was increased irritability, argumentativeness, and anger. We became concerned that the diagnosis of bipolar disorder was being missed. After discussions with the parents and psychiatrist, we all agreed to try a mood stabilizer, lithium, for the highs and lows we were seeing, and the SSRI medication was discontinued. There was a modulation in mood over several weeks with lithium. During this time the ADHD medication was continued to help treat his distractibility in school.

This case was interesting in several respects. We came upon the bipolar diagnosis slowly. It has often been the case that bipolar disorder is not picked up immediately in children and adolescents. Until recently, it was thought to be a problem mainly for adults. In addition, ADHD is a more prevalent disorder and has some overlapping symptoms with bipolar disorder. Thus, it is not unusual to try ADHD medications first if a child has difficulty with distractibility and impulsivity. It is important for parents and doctors to consider a thorough evaluation for bipolar disorder if the child is so revved up and so focused on immediate pleasure that he is uncontrollable at times in school and at home. In these situations, ADHD medication will have little or no effect. In fact in some situations, it can make a bipolar child even more out of control.

When Nothing Seems to Work

In Chapter 2, we also introduced you to a younger child, Edward, who had major problems with anger and impulse control. In Edward's case SSRIs and ADHD medications were tried first to control his anger and impulsivity at home and school. When a child is so wound up that he is kicking and hitting others on a regular basis when he is disciplined, why was medication for bipolar disorder not considered sooner? It is partly owing to the difficulty of accurately diagnosing bipolar disorder in young children. Because ADHD is much more common than bipolar illness in children, doctors usually treat ADHD first. The problem is that ADHD medications by themselves will generally not work if the child also has moderate to severe bipolar symptoms. In Edward's case, the impulsivity got even more out of control when stimulant medications were tried.

After the ADHD medications and SSRIs were discontinued, Edward was tried on risperidone (Risperdal), which is in a class of medications known as "atypical antipsychotics" (see Table 6.3). These medications are newer and different in action than the older antipsychotics. The atypical antipsychotics (risperidone, olanzapine, quetiapine, ziprasidone, clozapine) are usually preferred over the older antipsychotics, because they are easier to tolerate owing to their few side effects. They help reduce agitation, irritability, impulsivity, argumentativeness, and the "revved up" behavior of bipolar children. The antipsychotic medications have traditionally been used with psychotic patients (patients who have hallucinations and delusions), but they are effective for treating pediatric bipolar disorder as well. There are some possible side effects, the most common being weight gain and tiredness. In Edward's case, he gained twenty pounds in several months. Another approach was needed.

TABLE 6.3 Atypical and Commonly Used Antipsychotics

Medication	Pediatric Dose	How Supplied	Mechanism of Action	Warnings
Aripiprazole (Abilify)	10–30 mg/day	Trade tablets: 5, 10, 15, 20, 30 mg	Unique modulation of dopamine; D2, D4, 5-HT2A antagonism and D2, 5-HT1A partial agonism‡	Metabolized by CYP3A4 and CYP2D6 so adjust dose for inducers or inhibitors of CYP3A4 and/or CYP2D6
Clozapine (Clozaril)	12.5–900 mg/day divided bid*; usual dose 300–450 mg/day divided bid*	Generic/trade tablets: 25, 100 mg	Serotonin and dopamine receptor antagonism	Agranulocytosis; WBC (white blood cell) counts weekly for first 6 months of treatment, then every 2 weeks; low extrapyradimal side effect risk
Olanzapine (Zyprexa)	2.5–20 mg qhs†	Trade tablets: 2.5, 5, 7.5, 10, 15, 20 mg	Serotonin and dopamine receptor antagonism	Weight gain; sedation; low extrapyradimal side effect risk
Quetiapine (Seroquel)	25–750 mg/day divided bid*	Trade tablets: 25, 100, 200 mg	Serotonin and dopamine receptor antagonism	Eye exam for cataracts every 6 months; low extrapyradimal side effect risk
Risperidone (Risperdal)	0.25–4 mg bid*	Trade tablets: 0.25, 0.5, 1, 2, 3, 4 mg; oral solution: 1 mg/ml	Serotonin and dopamine receptor antagonism	Weight gain; low extrapyradimal side effect risk; metabolized by CYP2D6
Ziprasidone (Geodon)	20–80 mg bid*	Trade caps: 20, 40, 60, 80 mg	Serotonin and dopamine receptor antagonism	Somnolence; orthostatic hypotension; QT prolongation on electrocardiogram; metabolized by CYP3A4

* morning and evening dosing
† at bedtime
‡ combining with receptors to cause drug action

Using Mood Stabilizers

Few studies have been done to examine the treatment of mania in children and adolescent patients. In clinical practice, we use similar medications for children and adults (see Table 6.4). Lithium is the only medication that has been approved by the FDA for the treatment of mania in adolescents. This is because carefully "controlled" studies have been done showing its effectiveness with adolescents, but not yet with children ages twelve and under. A "controlled" study is one in which patients are divided randomly into two groups; one group gets the active medication, and the other gets a sugar pill, or placebo. If the medication is shown to help better than the placebo, then we feel more confident that the medication is effective.

We are still using lithium and other mood stabilizers with children because these medications do help children, but the medications need to be monitored regularly for effectiveness and for side effects. There needs to be periodic blood levels done in a laboratory because lithium works within a therapeutic range of 0.8 to 1.2 mEq of lithium per liter of blood serum. If the blood level is too high, there can be serious side effects, and if the dose is too low, the treatment will be ineffective. Laboratory tests include renal (kidney) and thyroid function as well as lithium levels. We need to check laboratory values to see how much medication is in the blood serum and also to make sure there are no serious side effects to the kidney or thyroid. Even at lower levels of medication there can be side effects such as weight gain, acne, nausea, polydipsia (excessive thirst), polyuria (excessive urination), and tremor (shaking of some part of the body). If these side effects do not subside in the first few weeks, then the dosage will need to be decreased or the medication discontinued. Patients should avoid dehydration and salt restriction when taking lithium. What doctors and parents must weigh are the potential benefits versus the side effects. If the medication works well, and the side effects are mild, then the medication will be continued. If not, an alternative mood stabilizer will be considered.

TABLE 6.4 Mood Stabilizers

Medication	Pediatric Dose	How Supplied	Mechanism of Action	Warnings
Carbamazepine (Tegretol; Carbatrol)	100–1,000 mg/day, divided bid*	Generic tablets: 200 mg; chewable 100 mg; trade extended release tablets: 100, 200, 300, 400 mg; suspension: 100 mg/5 ml	Unclear	Aplastic anemia; CYP3A4 induction
Lamotrigine (Lamictal; Lamictal CD)	25–200 mg/day	Trade tablets: 25, 100, 150, 200 mg; chewable tablets: 5, 25 mg	Unclear	Severe, potentially life-threatening rashes (Stevens-Johnson syndrome) in .8% of children; multiple drug interactions via CYP450
Lithium (Lithobid; Eskalith)	200–1,800 mg/day divided bid*; steady state in 5 days; trough levels for maintenance 0.6–1.2 mEq/L, for acute mania 1.0–1.5 mEq/L	Generic/trade capsules: 150, 300, 600 mg; tablets: 300 mg; trade extended release tablets: 300, 450 mg; syrup: 300 mg/5 ml	Unclear	Monitor renal and thyroid function; avoid dehydration, NSAIDS, salt restriction; ACE inhibitors and diuretics increase levels
Valproic acid (Depakene; Depakote)	10–15 mg/kg/day; titrate to maximum 60 mg/kg/day	Generic tablets: 250 mg; trade sprinkles: 125 mg; extended release tablets: 125, 250, 500 mg; syrup: 250 mg/5 ml	Unclear	Hepatotoxicity; drug interactions

* morning and evening dosing

Divalproex sodium (Depakote) and valproic acid (Depakene) also can be used as a mood stabilizer for treatment of manic episodes. Divalproex sodium usually is started at a dose of 20 mg/kg/day. Again blood levels are taken, and the optimal blood level is between 80 and 120 ug/ml. Potential side effects include weight gain, sedation, tremor, and nausea. These side effects occur in between 10 to 20 percent of cases. In females, there may be an increased risk of menstrual irregularities and polycystic ovary disease. In polycystic ovary disease, a hormonal imbalance leads to ovarian cysts, hairiness, and weight gain. If side effects do not diminish after the initial week of treatment, the dosage of divalproex is reduced or discontinued. The other medication, valproic acid, also can cause serious side effects in a small number of cases. Life-threatening cases of pancreatitis have been reported in patients taking valproic acid. If patients develop pancreatitis, thrombocytopenia (low platelets), or liver dysfunction, the medication should be discontinued immediately. Additionally, it is important for the doctor to be aware of the many drug interactions that can occur with divalproex and valproic acid through the liver's cytochrome P450 isoenzyme system. If other medications are being taken that affect the same enzyme system, then the dosages of one of the medications may need to be altered.

Carbamazepine (Carbatrol, Tegretol, and Tegretol XR) is used less commonly than lithium or valproic acid for children with bipolar disorder. Initially the dose is increased to 15 mg/kg/day. The optimal blood level is 7 to 10 ug/ml. Potential side effects include nausea, sedation, hyponatremia (low sodium level), rash, aplastic anemia (the bone marrow stops making blood cells), and Stevens-Johnson syndrome (blisters form on skin and mucous membranes). The latter two are extremely serious, and carbamazepine should be discontinued immediately if these occur. A complete blood count (CBC) including platelets and liver enzymes (LFTs) should be monitored periodically in all patients taking carbamazepine. Similar to divalproex and valproic acid, it is important for the doctor to be aware of the many drug interactions that can occur with carbamazepine through the liver's cytochrome P450 isoenzyme system.

Lamotrigine (Lamictal and Lamictal CD) is also used for children with bipolar disorder. This medication, however, requires caution in children because of the 0.8 percent risk of the development of severe, potentially life-threatening rashes in children (Stevens-Johnson syndrome or toxic epidermal necrolysis). The risk in adults is lower, approximately 0.3 percent. This medication should be discontinued at the first sign of rash. Lamotrigine also requires dose adjustment when given with antiepileptic drugs, such as carbamazepine and valproic acid, because all these medications affect the liver enzymes.

Order of Medications for Bipolar Disorder and ADHD

One question that has not yet been resolved in the treatment of children with bipolar disorder and ADHD is whether to start with an atypical antipsychotic medication or a mood stabilizer. Sometimes, as in the case of Edward, an antipsychotic is tried first, and, in some cases, a mood stabilizer is used first. We prefer starting with an antipsychotic in cases where there are rapid shifts of mood in a single day. Most of the children we see do not stay in a manic phase for more than a few hours. While a mood stabilizer can be used in these cases, an antipsychotic works faster and there is no need for blood draws as there is with mood stabilizers. The blood draws are needed with mood stabilizers to check on the amount of medication that is in the blood serum and to make sure there are no serious side effects. Side effects can be extremely serious with mood stabilizers, though they are rare.

For many of the children who have bipolar disorder and ADHD, neither a mood stabilizer alone nor an antipsychotic alone seems to resolve all of the problems. Each medication seems to quiet some of the "revved up" behaviors in many of these children, but often there continue to be impulsivity and attention problems. In one small study of bipolar adolescents, some of whom had also been diagnosed with ADHD and some of whom had not, it was found that those teenagers who had a history of ADHD did not improve as much on lithium as the group who only had bipolar disorder. About a third of the dual-diagnosis cases did not respond to lithium, whereas only 10 percent of teens with bipolar disorder alone did not respond. In another preliminary study with a small number of dual-diagnosis cases, the effectiveness of an atypical antipsychotic, risperidone, was evaluated. The antipsychotic medication was effective for manic symptoms, but not ADHD symptoms.

We are finding that sometimes treatment with two or more medications is necessary for children and adolescents with bipolar disorder and ADHD. For some children, when a mood stabilizer helps only in part, and there continue to be problems with impulsivity and "revved up behaviors," the addition of an atypical antipsychotic is effective. Recent studies with adolescents have supported this combination for treatment of adolescent mania. We have also found this to be effective in a few cases of bipolar disorder and ADHD.

This approach is what was ultimately found to be helpful for Edward. When taking a mood stabilizer with an antipsychotic medication, Edward usually did not lose control of his anger. Hitting and kicking stopped. There was still some swearing at his parents, especially when he was tired. In school, he was able to ignore provocative students most of the time, and he no longer touched other students inappropriately to get their attention. Overall, he was calmer, less impulsive, and more focused in school. Because both his bipolar and ADHD symptoms had improved, and because he previously had a poor response to ADHD medications, no ADHD medications were added to the treatment regimen.

In other children with ADHD and bipolar illness, stimulant medication may be gradually added to treat distractibility, if that symptom continues, once there has been successful treatment of mood problems with the appropriate mood stabilizer and/or antipsychotic. Depending on the response, the ADHD medications become part of the treatment regimen. ADHD medications are often needed, but they are effective only after mood stabilization with appropriate medication for mania.

Children and adolescents with bipolar illness and ADHD usually remain on their medications for several years. In the only maintenance treatment study for pediatric bipolar disorder, patients who continued to take lithium had a significantly lower relapse rate than patients who stopped taking it. When children or adolescents with bipolar disorder have been without symptoms for several years, the mood stabilizer and/or antipsychotic medication can be tapered gradually over several months and then be discontinued. If symptoms recur, then the medications should be restarted.

The treatment of bipolar illness and ADHD is a new and exciting area, where we are beginning to see significant responses to the use of several medications in combination. Larger studies are needed to validate this new approach. One reason that larger research studies have not been done yet is that we are still working on defining the necessary diagnostic features of these children. At present, researchers at different institutions may classify dual-diagnosis children differently. Another factor that delays extensive research of these medications in dual-diagnosis children is that the work on pediatric bipolar disorder itself (when no ADHD is present) is still in its infancy. Only in the last few years have researchers begun to look at bipolar disorder and its treatment in children. Clinicians must often act before all the research data is complete because children with bipolar disorder and ADHD have such major difficulties at home and in school, and psychotherapeutic interventions without medication have little lasting effect in these children. Once medications have lessened the severity of these children's symptoms, psychotherapy helps teach more appropriate alternatives for expressing anger and helps these children develop social skills.

CHAPTER 7

ADHD and Behavioral Disorders

Children Who Fight the Rules

Does your child argue with you constantly about your requests to do homework, to come home on time, to get ready for bed, and more? Do you find yourself yelling or punishing your child every day? One common diagnosis that can coexist with ADHD is oppositional defiant disorder. These children are frequently hostile when parents try to set rules. The problem can occur with authorities at school as well. Research studies show that at least 35 percent of children with ADHD also have oppositional defiant disorder (ODD). In some studies, the percentage with ODD was as high as 65 percent.

Mary: Passive Resistance

Mary was seven years old when she came in with her mother and father. "I can't get her to get ready in the morning," explained her mother. "When I try to enforce something, Mary refuses to cooperate." The mother explained she had to prod and argue with Mary every step of the way: waking up, brushing teeth, getting dressed, having breakfast. Her mother was extremely frustrated. The mother was mild mannered and shy by nature and could not deal with arguing with her daughter every morning. Owing to Mary's procrastination, she was late to school by about fifteen minutes most mornings. Mary did not yell or use foul language; she would passively resist by refusing to get ready until her mother was close to a rage.

The same pattern continued at home after school with homework and bedtime. Whenever the child did not want to do something, she resisted quietly, but strongly. It was exhausting for her parents. There was not this level of disobedience in school. Mary was reasonably well-behaved and avoided disciplinary action in school, though her work was inconsistent. The teacher reported that Mary was easily distracted by other things going on in the room. In addition, her folders were poorly organized, and she had difficulty finding her homework papers to turn in. But these problems were owing to ADHD (which Mary had already been diagnosed with), not oppositionality.

Mary, unlike some oppositional children, cared more about the rules and consequences in school. The fact that she was mostly compliant in school was a clue that the parents needed to impose a system similar to what her teacher was using. Another interesting feature in this case was the absence of severe arguments. Mary's oppositionality was more passive. In other cases, children's oppositional behavior is more loud and aggressive, and often problems with following adult rules are apparent both in school and at home.

Jimmy and David: Repeated Pranks Turn Off Others

Two examples of this more aggressive form of ODD are Jimmy and David. Jimmy was diagnosed with ADHD when he was seven years old and came in for therapy at age eight because his ADHD medication was not working well. His mother explained, "Jimmy has tantrums when he does not get his way." As an example, his mother (a single parent) described difficulties she had shopping with her children: Jimmy and his brother did not stay with her in the store, and she had to keep insisting that they not stray too far. Jimmy's older brother sometimes violated his mother's rules, but not nearly as often as Jimmy. The brother was usually compliant, while Jimmy was more headstrong and often ignored his mother's requests to stay near her in the store. In one situation, his mother took away the privilege of going to a fast-food restaurant as a consequence for Jimmy's behavior in a store. Jimmy erupted in the car. "He kicked the door hard, and he actually managed to open it while I was driving. He stopped when I threatened to spank him."

Jimmy also made disrespectful remarks at times toward his teachers. Jimmy once said "that's dumb," and another time "poop," when he did not like what the teacher asked him to do. He talked a lot during class and frequently did not complete his work in school.

David, age twelve, came for therapy with no preliminary diagnosis, and he had some behavior problems that were even more severe than Jimmy's. He pinched several girls in school on the buttocks and took money from his parents' wallets. David thought the pinching was funny, and he thought that it was a strategy to get the other boys in his class to like him. He did not seem to realize how offended the girls would feel about his behavior. Though he was punished, including a school suspension, he repeated this behavior a few more times over the next few months. The other boys in his class did not like him much before he did this, and things did not improve with his peers afterward. The lack of peer response and the increasing consequences at home and school led him to stop this kind of behavior.

Stealing his parents' money was another attempt to curry favor with his classmates. He gave some of this money to the children in his class in the hopes that they would like him. The previous year he had taken candy from the teacher's desk and given it to his classmates after school. David had much difficulty making friends, and he did not realize that his giving away money and candy would not help. It seemed that his peers avoided him because he was impulsive and not attentive to them. They were also put off by his immature verbal humor and his inconsistency in listening to them.

Tom: Resistance in the Late Teen Years

Tom liked to challenge his parents' rules and beliefs. He was eighteen and argued regularly with his parents about their rules about not smoking in the house and about staying away from pot and alcohol. The arguing would lead to even larger debates about morality, religion, and why work was important in life. But no matter how often his parents insisted he not smoke or drink in the house, Tom would do what he wanted whenever he thought his parents would not be home. Then they would return home often to find Tom smoking or drinking with his friends. There would be a loud argument, during which some consequence was imposed, such as taking away his car privileges. Tom would storm out of the house. He would make an effort during the next week or two to earn back car privileges. However, his lack of regard for his parents' wishes would then return. It was a chronic problem. Owing to the frequent, almost daily, arguments about a variety of subjects, and because Tom made little or no effort to avoid these confrontations, it was more difficult for Tom's parents to deal with Tom than their other adolescent child who occasionally violated their rules.

Tom did well academically in high school because he was bright and could do well on most tests without studying. If he forgot to bring something to school, his parents would help out and bring it to him, or teachers would give him an extra day. He was a straight A student in high school even though he did little homework. However, this approach did not work well in college, where he had to write research papers and take harder tests. Tom was disorganized and did no schoolwork until the last minute, and as a result, his grades plummeted. His use of marijuana and alcohol "to chill" increased. It was during his freshman year in college when he was in danger of failing out of school that he first came to a psychiatrist for help.

Ned: Disrespectfulness Escalates to Violating the Law

Ned did not have the cognitive gifts that Tom had, and his motivation was a serious problem in junior high and high school. By the time Ned was in high school, he was truant once a week or more. He would miss important tests and then receive failing grades. He would be defiant with teachers he did not like. "One teacher was an ass; she didn't want to pass me, so I just left." With another teacher, "The bell was about to ring [signaling the end of class], so I left, and the teacher gave me a detention. She wrote I left five minutes early. No way." Ned always found fault with adult authority, never with his own behavior.

Ned had problems with authorities in the community as well. The police stopped him and his friends several times because they were drinking in a park. The drinking increased to the point that he experienced a blackout (that is, the next day he did not remember much of what had happened). He regularly violated his parents' rules about drinking and curfew. Twice his parents threw him out of the house for several days. Finally, his antisocial behavior progressed to stealing food and cigarettes from a local store and throwing eggs at cars and houses at night. He was caught stealing, and his case was assigned to the juvenile court system. It was around this time Ned came for therapy. He had been on ADHD medications for a number of years, but his behaviors had only worsened.

Defining Behavior Disorders

The *DSM-IV* (1994) defines oppositional defiant disorder (ODD) as "a recurrent pattern of negativistic, defiant, disobedient, and hostile behavior toward authority figures that persists for at least six months." Examples of oppositional behavior given in *DSM-IV* include often losing temper, often arguing with adults, often refusing to comply with adults' requests, often blaming others, and often being vindictive. Notice that the diagnostic manual uses the word "often." One or two outbursts or occasionally defiant behavior is not enough to be classified as ODD. Many teens occasionally defy adult rules, but they do not have ODD. There needs to be a repeated pattern of defiance to be oppositional defiant disorder.

Another more serious coexisting problem for many ADHD children is conduct disorder (CD). With conduct disorder, there is not just arguing and defiance with adults, but major societal rules are broken, such as aggression toward people and animals, destruction of property, or theft (*DSM-IV*). For younger children these problems are usually evident in frequent fighting and intimidation of other children, shoplifting, or lying to obtain objects or favors from others. It is important to know that an occasional school-yard fight or lying to avoid chores is not a conduct disorder. There must be a consistent pattern of violation of societal rules and the rights of others over at least a year.

For adolescents, conduct disorder may take the form of more serious fighting with weapons, burglary of expensive items, or running away from home and truancy (*DSM-IV*). These adolescents have often been to juvenile court and have had dealings with the local police. One trip to the police or court does not qualify for the diagnosis of conduct disorder. As in the case of younger children with the disorder, there needs to be a *regular* pattern of violation of societal rules. Studies find that between 30 to 50 percent of children with ADHD also have conduct disorders. Some of these studies of conduct disorder also include children who have oppositional defiant disorder. The percentage of ADHD children and adolescents who truly have conduct disorder is probably below 30 percent. Still, these figures show that conduct disorder is a frequent co-occurring condition with ADHD.

In our case examples, David and Ned showed signs of a conduct disorder with ADHD, while Mary, Jimmy, and Tom had ADHD and oppositional defiant disorder. The difference between the two kinds of cases was that David and Ned showed a disregard for societal rules and the rights of others. Remember how

David pinched girls' butts several times, though he was told each time this was a violation of school rules and a violation of the girls' rights to have control over their own bodies. He also stole money and candy. David did not get into frequent arguments with his parents and teachers as children with oppositionality disorder usually do; he instead did what he wanted to do regardless of the feelings of adults and regardless of the rules of society. Similarly, Ned broke a number of societal rules: he was truant, he drank to excess, he stole, and he defaced property. Tom, who was similar in age to Ned, drank like Ned did, but he did not disregard most of society's rules. He showed some awareness and concern about societal expectations, as he did not drink in public and he did not steal or deface property.

Taken together these diagnoses are often labeled behavior disorders because they have to do with problem behaviors, rather than difficulties with mood. There might be some irritability and negative mood with behavior-disorder children but not to the degree that exists with depression or bipolar disorders. There is a continuum from oppositional defiant disorder to conduct disorder. With ODD, there is often arguing with parents, while with CD children there are violations not only of parental rules but also of society's rules. There are many ODD children who never develop a conduct disorder; however, most conduct-disordered children have at one time had characteristics of ODD. Many of the studies of dual diagnosis with ADHD group the diagnoses of ODD and CD together.

Distinguishing Behavior Disorders from Depression

It is important to distinguish between behavior disorders and mood disorders, though occasionally both can be present. The treatment will be different depending on the diagnosis. With depression, there is not only irritability but also generally a decrease in energy and interest in doing things, which is not the case with behavior disorders. In addition, with depression, the child or adolescent may have some feelings of hopelessness or worthlessness, whereas with behavior disorders there are more often displays of cockiness and power.

What makes distinguishing depression from behavior disorders so difficult sometimes is that children and adolescents who are depressed often do not express their unhappiness in "adult" language. That is, the child or adolescent may not speak of hopelessness or of decreased energy. If depressed children spoke this way, it would be easier to make the diagnosis of depression. Observations by parents and teachers are often critical to determine whether there has been a significant decrease in involvement in school or home activities. If there is a withdrawal from activities with other people, it is usually a sign of decreased energy and depression.

One of the more prevalent symptoms in both depressed and oppositional youth is increased irritability. In fact, at first glance it is easy for parents and clinicians to think that their irritable and disagreeable children are oppositional. How does the parent or doctor know if irritability is a sign of depression or of oppositional disorder? Before deciding, it is important to consider how pervasive the child's challenging of adults is—this is essential to distinguish between the two disorders. With depressive disorders, there is arguing only when the child is moody, whereas with oppositionality these arguments are pretty regular, almost everyday, and can last for as long as the adult is present. It is important therefore to consider the timing of the arguments. If they occur only when the child is moody and if the arguments are of recent origin do not be too quick to rule out depression. Consider also the child's level of interest in school and home activities, and think carefully about the history of mood disorders in your family tree. Remember in cases of depression there is usually a family history of mood problems. If there is a family history of depression and if parents or teachers notice a pullback in the child's interest or commitment to activities, it is likely that the child is exhibiting depression and not oppositional defiant disorder.

In our examples, the oppositional children argued frequently, usually daily, with adults. Mary resisted her parents several times a day: when getting ready in the morning, when it was time to do homework, and at bedtime. Her defiance was more passive, but just as frequent and just as aggravating to her parents as if she had been more vocal. Jimmy was more vocal about his daily disagreements with his mother. In addition, Jimmy had conflicts with teachers. As you can see, the duration and frequency of the arguing is greater for oppositionality compared with depression.

Conduct disorders are more easily distinguished from depressive disorders by virtue of the instances in which societal rules are broken. Depressed children generally do not break society's rules, whereas conduct-disorder children do.

Distinguishing Behavior Disorders from Bipolar Disorder

Distinguishing conduct disorder from bipolar disorder is not that easy. Both types of children break society's rules. Both types of children pursue their own interests even if society has rules that dictate otherwise. However, what is usually different is the motivation and emotionality of the children. Bipolar children are excited and revved up when they break rules, whereas conduct-disorder children often exhibit coolness and an unemotional demeanor. Bipolar children are seeking immediate pleasure, whereas conduct-disorder children are usually more interested in power or material gain. Conduct-disordered children are more calculating when they break societal rules because they are interested in exhibiting their power over others or interested in gaining some financial reward.

In our examples, the bipolar children (discussed in Chapter 2) touched others in order to receive physical and emotional stimulation, whereas the conduct-disordered adolescent Ned wanted material things like tobacco products or threw eggs in a display of power and anger. David, a conduct-disordered preadolescent, did engage in touching behavior; however, it was not for immediate pleasure. He thought it would show his peers how cool and powerful he was. Again, the main goal of the conduct-disordered child is usually power or material gain, while the main goal of the bipolar child is generally immediate emotional excitement. If it is difficult to determine the child's motivation, look for the overall level of emotionality displayed by the child or adolescent. The excessive emotionality of the bipolar child is very different from the coolness and emotional reserve usually displayed by the conduct-disordered child. That is the most obvious difference between cases of conduct disorder and bipolar disorder.

The emotionality of the bipolar child is also useful when distinguishing this diagnosis from oppositionality disorder. Both types of children argue with adults, often on a daily basis. What is different is what preceded the arguments as well as the emotionality with which they are expressed. Bipolar children get angry when their pleasure-seeking behavior is interrupted. Otherwise they can be quite cooperative with adults, whereas oppositional children usually are angry whenever adult rules are imposed. Also, the anger of bipolar children is more dramatic and explosive, whereas oppositional children can be quite lawyerlike in their disagreements.

In summary, there are two main diagnostic groups that fall under the behavior disorders category: oppositional defiant disorder (ODD) and conduct disorder (CD). For ODD, there are often frequent arguments with parents and/or teachers but not serious violations of social norms, the latter being characteristic of CD. When one of these disorders occurs with ADHD, there are usually problems in school and at home more severe than with ADHD alone. Behavior disorders can be distinguished from mood disorders by the absence of severe fluctuations in energy. Depressed children exhibit low energy, while bipolar children have displays of heightened emotionality.

Interaction of ADHD with Behavior Disorders

There are two different theories about how ADHD and behavior disorders come to exist together. One theory is that ADHD comes first. An ADHD child often has problems with organization in school and frequently forgets assignments or books. As a result, this child is frequently disciplined by teachers and/or parents. After years of negative feedback from adults, the child may develop oppositional patterns of behavior. In other words, what started as forgetfulness becomes a bad habit of defying the parent's rules even when the rules have not been forgotten. It is as if the child is so used to being yelled at that he decides not to bother following the rules at all. What is one more argument, the child might reason. In fact, the child may come to enjoy the arguments. After all, negative attention is still attention, and children like to have the attention of their parents.

This theory would call for parents to vary their response to an ADHD child's forgetfulness, rather than respond always with criticism or anger. Parents do not want to fall into the rut of yelling at their ADHD child if this could contribute to the development of oppositional behavior or conduct disorders. Most parents will acknowledge that they are more negative with their ADHD children than with their non-ADHD children. While there are probably some children who develop behavior disorders secondarily to ADHD, similar to the pattern we have just outlined, there are many other children who seem to have both disorders beginning about the same time. After all, if the first theory were always true, then would not most ADHD children develop behavior disorders, because most parents frequently get angry with their ADHD children?

The second theory is that ADHD and behavior disorders are formed independently and occur around the same time. Once these two disorders are both present, there will probably be some interaction between them. If a child is forgetful owing to ADHD, he is going to receive more negative feedback from adults, and there will be more frequent power struggles possible with adult authorities. The power struggles may affect the ADHD symptoms, like inattentiveness, in return. For example, Jimmy and Mary would tune out their parents sometimes out of anger.

As parents get worn down after so many struggles, typical ADHD issues, like disorganization at school or home, may not be worked on because they seem the least of the problems. For example, if a child is forgetting to bring home books and also getting into fights on the playground, parents and teachers are naturally going to be more concerned with the fights and not pay as much concern to the schoolwork. Thus, ADHD problems, like failing to finish or turn in homework, may continue unabated. The longer this happens, the harder it becomes to alter these academic habits. The result is a child with significant academic problems.

ADHD children who have behavior disorders present some different personality characteristics in therapists' offices compared to children with only ADHD. Often dual-diagnosis children seem more strong-willed and defiant from an early age. Parents report problems caring for these children as infants, long before there were problems with homework! In addition, these children often chose rougher, more defiant, friends. It makes it difficult for parents to enforce rules when their child's friends seemingly have no rules at home and violate rules in the community as well. The combination of peer influences and the early formation of a strong-willed personality make it likely that the child will exhibit behavior disorders.

Family Therapy

One key for parents is to work together with each other and with other relatives caring for the child as much as possible. Behavior-disorder children will try to find a loophole or try to divide parents. It is critical for you to discuss your game plan with your spouse on a regular basis to make sure that you stay united. If you face a problem while your spouse is away from home, it is fine for you to delay a response, if there is no immediate crisis, until after the two of you can speak with each other.

In the case of David, a twelve-year-old child, the parents and the therapist discussed strategy first, and then they had a joint discussion with David about his pinching girls and stealing money from his parents' wallets. The parents explained what their concerns were and let David know what the consequences would be:

namely, grounding him for a week from computer games and from seeing his friends. They also explained that there could be problems with the police or juvenile authorities if the behavior continued outside the home. In essence, the parents set standards for David's behavior with appropriate consequences.

For Ned, the teenager who, with friends, stole from a convenience store and threw eggs at cars and houses in the neighborhood, it was important to let him explain why he was doing this. Listening is more important with older adolescents, because they are more likely to think about what you say if you have listened to them first. When Ned was speaking, we tried to listen for what was critical to him: it was being together with his friends, not the violation of society's rules. The therapist then asked Ned and his parents if anyone could think of a compromise so that Ned could meet his social needs without serious risk of getting in additional trouble. For example, limiting his contact with friends late at night, because this was when the trouble usually occurred, was one possibility. Another possible compromise would be to visit with his friends at his own house rather than in the neighborhood where the stealing and egg throwing had occurred. A third possibility would be to forbid the teenager from going to the convenience store where the items were stolen but not to forbid him from meeting his friends.

It is difficult to manage what your child does in his free time the older he gets. For example, you cannot follow him around and make sure he stays away from the store in question. However, you can try to find a compromise where your limits (e.g., no stealing or egg throwing), are more likely to be respected. Let your teenager know that if he is caught violating the compromise arrangement, there will be serious consequences.

The incentives and consequences you choose for respecting your limits are important. The incentives and consequences need to be short term and meaningful to your child. For example, if your younger child likes to play outside, or likes the computer, these activities can be lengthened or shortened on a given day depending on your child's behavior. For the teenage Ned, if he goes to the "off-limits" store despite his parents' efforts to make a compromise agreement, then his privileges to visit whichever friends were involved would be suspended for a period of time. Because the original offense was a major violation (i.e., stealing) then the consequences for breaking the agreement would be more serious. Whatever you pick as the incentive or consequence, it has to be something your child cares about and something you also can control without having to follow him around constantly. If the consequence is the computer, for example, and you will not be present after school, you could remove the mouse or some necessary component. For Ned, it might be difficult to make the store off limits, unless the store owner agreed to call if Ned appeared.

For the younger child, you should not discuss the problem much with him but rather set a limit and use meaningful incentives and consequences to back up your limit. Words are not as effective as consequences for most children, especially younger ones. Keep your words short, and then change the subject or leave the room. Ignoring the child's complaints about the consequences and changing the subject are tools parents can use sometimes, and they may be just as effective in changing behavior as taking away television time. By ignoring your child, you will be withdrawing your attention, which is a meaningful negative consequence for many children.

With children who have ADHD and behavior disorders, it is important to set only a few goals to work on at a time. If you focus on too much, the child will be less likely to remember what he needs to change. Once one or two goals are accomplished, you can shift your focus to another.

Another important principle is to help your child to find a niche where he can be admired and active—a recommendation very similar to one we made for children with mood disorders. This suggestion is useful for children who could use a boost in self-esteem. For the young teen David, his parents involved him in a hockey league, because he liked physical activity and loved to skate. In this activity, there is also peer interaction that is supervised by adults—coaches and referees. If the child has some skill in the area all the better, as now the child will be receiving positive feedback, which will help his self-esteem.

Goals of Individual Psychotherapy

In addition to helping you develop these strategies, the psychologist will also try to build a bridge with your child or adolescent. Individual therapy is especially useful with the older child or adolescent who can reflect on the purposes of his misbehavior. The psychologist tries to understand the purposes of the older child's behavior and also tries to explain the purposes of the parent's behavior to the child or adolescent. If the underlying goals of the child and parent can be determined, there is a better chance of finding common ground and a behavior plan that will work. The behavior plan may not be totally acceptable to the child or adolescent, but if it has his or her input and recognizes his goals, there is a better chance of it succeeding.

Another purpose of developing rapport with these children is that it helps to build self-esteem if another adult listens and admires their thinking. These children have had such difficulty bonding with adults, owing to their disregard for adult rules, that they are often surprised that an adult really listens and tries to understand them. Once some rapport is established, it is also important for the therapist to be able to challenge the teen's behavior if it violates social norms. One way to do this is to point out the price the teen pays for his decision to break an important rule or law, such as the rule against physical fights in school. The therapist points out the cost, usually a school suspension, and wonders out loud how else the teen could let a classmate know to stop bothering him. The therapist would talk about using firm words or giving the cold shoulder, instead of fighting. The teen may not agree that the therapist's alternatives would be successful, and that's okay. True rapport is not just listening, nor is it achieved without listening. The skill and experience of the therapist helps him know when it is time to listen and accept the child's way of thinking and when it is time to challenge the child's assumptions or actions.

With the teenagers Ned and Tom, the therapist called them on their behavior when it violated social norms or when it provoked a major dispute with the parents that could have been avoided. With Ned, the therapist asked about the egg throwing, for example, and wondered aloud why he would risk so much trouble when he could have fun in other ways. With Tom, the therapist listened to his feelings about wanting to "chill" with his friends at home sometimes. The therapist then pointed out the costs if "chilling" meant smoking and drinking in the home when his parents were out. What were other alternatives that would not cost him so much goodwill with his parents? By asking these questions, or wondering aloud about the risks of some behaviors, the therapist is serving like an alter ego. The therapist thinks aloud on the teen's behalf, rather than becoming too judgmental about the behavior. There is implied criticism, but the effort is really to help the teen think through the costs and benefits of his behavior. The teen senses the therapist's caring attitude and is likely to consider his options more thoughtfully.

One final comment about psychotherapy with older children: because the therapist is meeting with the child alone as well as with the family, it is important at the outset to establish guidelines about confidentiality. Here is my approach: whatever the adolescent wants to keep private, I will honor as long as no one's life is in danger and as long as there is no child abuse. I suggest to the teenager that we discuss in family therapy those issues that are central to the conflicts within the family. I point out that this is bound to help the adolescent and the parents to understand each other and work out their differences. If the adolescent is concerned about doing this, I will wait until he is ready. If the child or adolescent does not want to discuss private information with me, because he is concerned I would share it with the parents, then a different therapist is suggested for either individual or family therapy.

It is the role of the therapist to shift between being a private listener to being a facilitator for the resolution of family problems. When working on the latter, it is important to support the parents in the adolescent's presence. If the therapist undercuts the parents, it will weaken their authority and set the therapist up as the ultimate family authority. In that case, the adolescent will try to use the therapy to get around family rules. If the therapist has concerns about the parents' behavior, it is best to discuss this with them alone.

Medication Issues

Oppositional children are often oppositional about their medication. It's advisable to help them see the value of the ADHD medication, and to pick a form of medicine that does not have to be administered multiple times a day, if possible. While the medication may help treat ADHD symptoms, like distractibility, it may not reduce some of the behavior problems, like arguing with adults. These problems are somewhat independent of the ADHD and thus independent of the ADHD medication.

Other medications may help with behavior disorders. Selection of the correct medication and optimal dose for each individual child with behavior disorders can be challenging. Without a specific medication approved by the FDA for the treatment of these disorders, parents must decide if the benefits of the off-label medications are worth the risks posed by their side effects. Often multiple medications are needed to adequately treat a child's combined diagnoses. Drug interactions, potential side effects, and duration of treatment are important considerations. The diverse medications available to treat behavior disorders that occur in a child who has ADHD include the ADHD psychostimulant medications in addition to the noradrenergic agents, antidepressants, mood stabilizers, and atypical antipsychotics. (In Chapters 1 and 6, there are tables for each of these categories of medications.)

If your ADHD child's hyperactivity, impulsivity, or oppositionality is not adequately controlled by the psychostimulant medication, addition of a second medication may be warranted. In the 1990s, guanfacine or clonidine were commonly used as supplemental medications to control behavior disorders. These noradrenergic agents work by activation of alpha 2a norepinephrine receptors at presynaptic neurons in the brain. The activation of the receptors decreases cortical arousal in the cerebral cortex and thereby decreases distractions for the child. Clonidine and guanfacine are short-acting medicines, so that they are usually administered several times a day, which isn't ideal for these children. The dose is started at a low level and may be gradually increased. Each time any of these medications is increased, it is important to monitor heart rate, blood pressure, and electrocardiograms in order to prevent any cardiac difficulties. After treatment for six months, the cardiac monitoring should be performed every six months thereafter.

Although the noradrenergic agents can be effective especially for hyperactivity and impulsivity, the use of the atypical antipsychotics (newer antipsychotics that are being used for agitation and similar symptoms) has become commonplace in the past few years owing to their significant efficacy not only for hyperactivity and impulsivity, but also for oppositionality. Because the atypical antipsychotics are more likely to help with oppositionality, and as there are less frequent side effects than with the noradrenergics, these medicines are being used more than the noradrenergics. The most commonly used atypical antipsychotics in children are risperidone (Risperdal), olanzapine (Zyprexa), and quetiapine (Seroquel). These medications may even help with cognitive efficiency, organization, and social relatedness. Risperdal is dosed twice daily, Zyprexa at bedtime, and Seroquel twice daily. Notice that another advantage of these medicines relative to the noradrenergics is that they do not have to be given as many times a day.

The other main class of medicines that is sometimes tried for oppositionality and ADHD is antidepressants. If there are problems with frustration tolerance or mood, then these medicines are sometimes tried before the atypical antipsychotics; otherwise the antipsychotics are tried first. The antidepressant medication that is usually tried first is bupropion (Wellbutrin). Bupropion acts via inhibition of dopamine reuptake into the neurons of the brain. Another antidepressant that can be tried is venlafaxine (Effexor).

This medication exerts its effect via inhibition of both serotonin and norepinephrine reuptake and sometimes helps with oppositionality, explosiveness, irritability, and depressed mood.

Other antidepressants also can help treat the ADHD child who has oppositional symptoms. The selective serotonin reuptake inhibitors (SSRIs) assist in treatment primarily through their beneficial effects on irritability and depressed mood. A final choice in the antidepressant category is the tricyclic antidepressant group that includes amitriptyline, desipramine, and imipramine. These medications can reduce irritability, aggression, impulsivity, and hyperactivity. Desipramine probably is the most effective of the tricyclic antidepressants for oppositionality and behavior problems through its effect on arousal. During the dosing of tricyclic antidepressants, the blood levels of the medication and electrocardiograms should be obtained; these tests should be repeated every six months thereafter. The tricyclics are used less often at the present time than they were ten years ago because of the need to monitor for cardiovascular side effects.

One other category of medications, the mood stabilizers, is tried if the earlier choices are not working. The mood stabilizers can alleviate mood lability/instability, irritability, and aggression. Lithium, valproic acid, and carbamazepine are the three most commonly used mood stabilizers for ADHD children with oppositionality. The reason these medicines are tried last is that side effects can be more serious. Periodic blood draws are required to monitor the level of the medication as well as the effects on the kidney and thyroid. (Refer to Chapter 6 for further explanation of the above medications.)

While there is increasing use of secondary medications in addition to psychostimulants when there are behavior disorders, it is important to remember that this approach is still somewhat controversial. There have not yet been major studies of their effectiveness. Our clinical experience suggests that these medicines only work sometimes for behavior disorders. It is often behavior modification and limit setting by parents in coordination with other adults that is critical. It is important for parents not to get discouraged when there are new problem behaviors at home or in the community. Work together with other adults to brainstorm how to manage these problems. What is the purpose of your child's behavior, and what have you used effectively in the past to modify other behaviors?

Day-to-Day Problems and How to Deal with Them

Let's review in more detail a few examples of behavioral problems and how you can work with your children to reduce violations of important rules.

Your Child Says He Does Not Have Homework or Argues Daily About Doing It

Children with ADHD and behavior disorders are even more resistant to homework than most ADHD children. They want to be free to see their friends or do other activities of their own choosing. There are several things you can try. One is to talk with your child's teacher about the problem, and come up with a plan together. The school is your ally, and it is important to keep that alliance strong. Keep in touch with the teacher in a way that is comfortable and easy for the teacher. Does the teacher like phone calls or some written system for communication? If you work together, it is more likely that you will be successful.

Another basic principle is to have a favorite activity be contingent upon completing the homework. With behavior-disorder children more than other ADHD children, it is critical that they not play outside or do what they want inside the house until they have done their homework. In this way you are creating a natural incentive to finish homework. If you cannot tell whether your child finished his homework, you need to rely on the teacher's feedback to you the next day, and there can be a consequence or incentive when you hear back from the teacher.

Another possibility for older children who are resistant to doing homework is to hire a tutor. This avoids a regular power struggle with you, and many adolescents are more cooperative with adults other than their parents. For many parents, though, cost is a factor. Sometimes a family friend or relative who lives near the home may be willing to help at little or no cost. The tutor in this case does not need to be an educational expert, as the problems are more behavioral than cognitive. The tutor needs to be someone who can form a relationship with adolescents. The tutor hopefully would also be willing to communicate with the teacher, which will help the adolescent realize that the tutor can find out what is going on if the adolescent tries to mislead him.

Your Younger Child Hits Other Children and Walks Away When the Teacher Disciplines Her

In this case, working on a behavior-modification system with the school is critical so that the child knows that all of the adults care about changing her behavior. In this example, we would recommend dividing the school day into periods and then rate two kinds of behavior for each class period: one behavior category would be talking respectfully to teachers, and the other would be playing with friends without hurting them. For each period, the teacher would mark a smile or frown on a sheet of paper, and at the end of the day the child would bring it home for her parents to see. There would be an activity incentive at home, such as going to the park or playing with a certain toy that "belongs" to the parents. (The toy would be in the parents' possession and would only be handed to the child for a certain time on days she had earned it.) The child would earn the incentive if she achieved a certain number of smiley faces in school. In addition, there would be a negative consequence if there were too few smiley faces. The consequence could be either no television or not going outside for the rest of the day, for example. Each day the behavior modification would start afresh, so that the child has a reason to try to control her behavior in school the following day.

Your Adolescent Refuses to Go to School and Sleeps Until Noon

Your child feels he cannot do well in his classes and wants to drop out. Before deciding on your response, it is important to determine first why your adolescent is sleeping and refusing to go to school. If the child is anxious or depressed, this needs to be treated with psychotherapy and/or medication. If you and your child's doctor rule out mood disorders and anxiety and feel the problem is more one of oppositionality, then it is important for you and the school together to discuss a course of action. What kind of negative consequence will be most meaningful to your adolescent? Do you or the school have the power to impose a consequence that the child cares about? For example, a suspension will not help if the child does not want to be in school anyway. At home, you could take away car privileges if the adolescent does not attend school on a given day, but if the adolescent has friends that can drive, he may not care much. In some cases, it may become necessary to notify juvenile authorities to meet with your child to let him know of possible court action if he does not attend school regularly. The bottom line with behavior-disorder children is that there needs to be some kind of consequence that is meaningful to them.

Sometimes there are significant learning problems the adolescent is having owing to his ADHD and poor attendance. Sometimes a reduced class load or an alternative school with smaller classes and more supervision may be useful. See what your school district offers. Most state laws require school districts to provide an alternative educational program, if your child cannot be successful in the regular program owing to a disability. ADHD and behavior problems qualify as a disability.

Your Child Repeatedly Steals Items from Stores and Takes Money from Your Purse or Wallet

Stealing is a serious problem with some adolescents who have ADHD and behavior problems. For repeat offenders, it is often necessary for real-world consequences to occur in order for the adolescent to realize the dangers of this behavior. It may be necessary to let courts take a punitive action, such as having the adolescent perform community service or, in cases of continuing theft, having your child go to a juvenile detention facility for a short time. Court action can be very difficult for parents, who often feel like a failure when this happens. Unfortunately, some children test society's limits despite parents' best efforts. For these adolescents there needs to be a higher authority that they hopefully do respect.

In your house, it will be important to reduce temptation by keeping your purse or wallet with you or in a locked area. Having to constantly keep track of your money in your own house is an unpleasant chore. However, it is important to realize that the problem is severe and needs severe actions both in your home and in the community to try to prevent the stealing from becoming a lifelong problem.

Another course of action would be to remove your adolescent from at least some of his friends. Often stealing is encouraged by these friends. How can you prevent your teenager from seeing certain friends? Make sure significant negative consequences occur when you find out your child violated your rules about who he can visit. It may even become necessary to send your adolescent to a different school out of the area (if the family can afford a private school, or if the courts are willing to impose this consequence). This will break the ties with his entire group of friends, but there are no guarantees that your adolescent will not find a similar group eventually at the new school. Thus, check out the schools in advance, and see what the student population is like and how well the students are supervised. Usually the more structured and active the school's programs, the more likely an adolescent with behavior disorders will improve.

CHAPTER 8

ADHD and Less Frequent Co-Occurring Diagnoses

Autistic Spectrum Disorders and Tic Disorders

Sometimes when a child has been treated for ADHD, there is some improvement in distractibility and hyperactive symptoms, but the parents and teachers notice that the child still acts in an unusual or odd manner. The characteristics fall into two main categories: lack of interest in peer interactions and restricted repertoire of interests or activities. The child usually prefers to play alone with a favorite toy rather than join other children in group activities. The isolation from peers was present even before treatment for ADHD was started, and it does not usually diminish with the use of stimulant medication. The problem we are describing falls into the spectrum of disorders known as autism or pervasive developmental disorders. What should parents do to help their child interact more normally with peers? Also, how do parents help these children become more flexible?

Another kind of problem that sometimes occurs with ADHD is tic disorders: tics can be facial grimacing or repeated jerking of one's arm, leg, or neck. Sometimes there are vocal tics, such as throat clearing or grunting. In some cases, tics do not appear until the ADHD child has been treated with stimulant medication. What should parents do about motor or vocal tics?

Kevin: Troubles with Peers

Kevin came for an evaluation when he was in kindergarten. He was not interacting well with other classmates; he often ignored them. If they interrupted something he was doing, Kevin would sometimes spit in their faces or throw sand at them. He would not sit down during story time or eat a snack with the others. When the children were supposed to leave for another room, the teacher had to hold his hand and guide him out the door; otherwise he would remain in the class.

At home when he was frustrated, he took a swing at his parents or banged on the piano. At meals, if he did not want to sit at the table, he would have a tantrum or throw his food on the floor. The rest of the evening he played with his toys alone or watched television. In the morning, his parents had to wake him several times and then help him get dressed and ready to leave for school. Usually he would ignore their instructions to get dressed; eventually his mother would have to hold him in her lap and help him put on his school clothes.

When he came to my office, he did not want to answer any questions, and he rarely looked at me. To establish a rapport with Kevin, I followed his lead. "Transformers" (plastic toys that change from one object to another that were popular five to ten years ago) fascinated him. He and I made up stories about the transformers, and, at those times, he was more responsive and looked at me. If I asked him a question about his activities at school or home, he would look away and basically ignore me. I encouraged his parents to interact with Kevin more at home by using toys that he liked. As a result, he became more interactive at home, played alone less, and actually began seeking out his parents to help make up stories about his toys. The stories were repetitive, with the same characters and same themes over and over again. It was boring for his parents, but I encouraged them to keep playing. I also suggested that they occasionally introduce a new theme or a new toy, and sometimes Kevin would accept the change. If he was interested in the new topic, it became a part of the story. There was gradually increasing interaction with his parents and gradually increasing variations in the stories they would tell. It was important to start with an activity that already interested Kevin and then build from there.

We also used a behavior-modification chart in order to reduce hitting, spitting, and throwing sand in school. A behavior-modification chart records the frequency of a behavioral goal for the child and indicates what the reward or consequence may be for that goal. For example, for Kevin the behavioral goal was self-control, rather than hitting, throwing sand, or spitting. We suggested Kevin use phrases like "stop it" if a child was bothering him, or he could let the teacher know. We divided the morning into the class periods and gave smiley faces for each period of time that Kevin exhibited self-control. We offered an activity reward in school; in Kevin's case, the reward was time to play with a couple of transformer toys, which the teacher kept unless Kevin earned time to use them. After a few weeks, we switched incentives; we substituted a daily time when Kevin could play in the local park after school if he showed self-control. The key was to pick incentives that Kevin really enjoyed and change the incentives when Kevin became bored with them. To make the behavior-modification plan even more powerful, his parents eventually added a consequence as well, namely taking away television time after school if the expectations were not reached.

It took several months to be effective, but eventually Kevin learned to use words (though loud and aggressive words) rather than physical actions when he was annoyed or interrupted by others. His impulsivity as well as his hyperactive behaviors continued. At the outset of therapy, we decided to focus on Kevin's lack of interaction with others and his inflexibility and defer any decisions about medication for possible ADHD. His parents were anxious about using medication, and in addition we wondered if his impulsive behaviors were a result of his social difficulties, rather than a sign of ADHD. After a year of improvements in social interaction, we tried a stimulant medication because Kevin's hyperactivity and impulsivity were not diminished. It was of modest help, and his parents decided to discontinue it. Kevin and his parents also took a break from therapy as we had achieved two of our main goals: there was no longer hostile physical behavior toward other children in school, and there was increasing social interaction with the parents at home.

Kevin returned to therapy in junior high school. At this time, he was belching in girls' faces, talking loudly and rudely at times to teachers, and rubbing his genitals during class. He was more interactive in therapy than he had been in kindergarten and first grade; however, when asked questions he did not want to answer, he walked over to the office toys and looked at them instead, so there was still a limit to Kevin's social responsiveness. Kevin's parents had been persistent about involving him in some social or athletic activity with other people. The activity that stuck was riding horses competitively. While Kevin did not always want to go to his lessons or competitions, his parents insisted. As a result, Kevin met new people at the competitions and also developed self-confidence. We believed his parents' insistence on some activity had helped Kevin's social development.

Though he was making some friends, he still exhibited some odd, and sometimes obnoxious, behaviors in his interactions with his classmates and friends, and as a result he was teased by some of the boys in his school. Therapy helped him to learn how these obnoxious behaviors (namely, belching in girls' faces or rubbing his genitals in class) were turning off people. Kevin began to curtail the belching and sexual behaviors in school. He also began talking appropriately on the phone and computer with several of the girls. These conversations were a remarkable shift away from his rude behavior. However, he had a tougher time being accepted by his male peers. There was one neighbor boy who, like Kevin, loved biking and Pokémon cards. They became good friends. But it was difficult for Kevin to make friends with the other boys at school because he was not interested in the sports activities that they liked. Also, he was teased for being "immature" when he tried to joke around with them: Kevin tended to make silly jokes about girls or talk about Pokémon cards, which most of the kids in his grade looked down upon. We took another break in therapy once he was consistently showing more appropriate behavior in school, though his social skills with peers still lagged. His parents decided to have Kevin work on these skills in group therapy with the social worker at his school.

What Is Pervasive Developmental Disorder?

Pervasive developmental disorder (PDD) is a relatively rare disorder occurring in about one in a thousand children according to some studies, or in five in a thousand children according to others. The two chief characteristics are severe impairment in social interaction skills and repetitive and stereotyped patterns of behavior (*DSM-IV*). The problems in social interaction can be manifested by inappropriate language or gestures, an absence of eye contact, lack of spontaneous interest in others, or a failure to develop peer relationships. The repetitive behaviors can range from head rocking and self-stimulation, which are more severe forms of stereotypical behavior, to preoccupation with a limited number of interests, such as wanting to play the same game alone everyday after school, rather than play outside with friends.

In its most severe form, PDD is known as autism. In these cases, there is also usually a failure to develop normal language and communication skills. At higher levels of functioning there is Asperger's syndrome, where language skills are intact, but there is still difficulty forming peer relationships, and the child exhibits a limited number of interests or activities. Finally, there is a category called PDD, not otherwise specified (PDD-NOS), where the deficits are not severe enough to fall under autism or Asperger's. However, problems with social interaction and rigid routines are still present. The PDD-NOS diagnosis is being increasingly used to describe those children who do not meet the full *DSM-IV* diagnostic criteria for autism and Asperger's syndrome. PDD-NOS children often prefer to play alone, but they are more likely than Asperger's children to form a meaningful friendship eventually in school. Notice that as the amount of social interaction increases, the diagnosis shifts: there is a lack of verbalizations in autism, an absence of significant peer interaction with Asperger's, and some peer interaction with PDD-NOS. Exactly where one draws the line between Asperger's and PDD-NOS is not established yet in the *DSM-IV* manual. Some clinicians use the Asperger's diagnosis more liberally and include many children that we, and other clinicians, would label PDD-NOS.

At the University of Chicago and other major centers for studying and treating autistic spectrum disorders, an observational rating scale is being used to make the diagnosis of autism, Asperger's, or PDD-NOS. The name of the scale is the "autism diagnostic observational schedule," or ADOS for short. The ADOS is especially helpful when the diagnosis of one of the autistic spectrum disorders is difficult to determine in a one-hour clinical interview. The ADOS uses "planned social occasions" carried out in the doctor's office to evaluate the child's social and communicative responses. The child's responses to these social situations are compared to the responses of other children. In this way, evaluators can determine if the child's behavior is more consistent with one diagnosis than with another.

It is the diagnosis of PDD-NOS that describes some of the behaviors seen in Kevin, our case example above. The difficulties that Kevin had with peers and the restricted number of interests he displayed continued over time. There were improvements, but not a total absence of symptoms at the junior high age. This is common in PDD-NOS children. Most mental-health professionals believe it is a genetic disorder that can be modified over time, but it does not usually disappear totally. It is important to recognize that the social skills problems are more severe for a child with PDD-NOS than for a child who has ADHD alone. Also, the problem is also not merely one of shyness. Shy children do not have tantrums nor do they hit others when they do not get their way.

ADHD and PDD: Can They Occur Together?

Many children with PDD are originally diagnosed as having ADHD instead. Distractibility, impulsivity, and social problems can be seen in both disorders. Because ADHD is a much more common disorder than PDD, parents and professionals may think a child has ADHD if they see any kind of hyperactivity or social issue, when the problem may really be PDD. There are important differences in the ways that symptoms like distractibility, impulsivity, and social problems are expressed in PDD, compared with ADHD.

Let's consider the symptom of distractibility first. A PDD child often becomes self-absorbed and is distracted more by internal thoughts and feelings than by people doing something nearby. The ADHD child, on the other hand, is more attuned to his surroundings and can be distracted not only by internal thoughts but also by external stimuli, such as other children talking or moving around in the room. Kevin showed both kinds of distractibility. Sometimes, he would stop doing what was being asked in class and tune in to his own thoughts. Other times, he would listen to others in the room, rather than do his work.

Impulsivity is another symptom that is seen in PDD and ADHD children. With ADHD, the impulsivity is an outgrowth of the child's being so active. The child has difficulty waiting, and he often interrupts others. For the PDD child, impulsivity is usually less frequent and occurs when the child is prevented from carrying on with his routine. The child may impulsively strike out in anger at these times. Another possible scenario for the PDD child is that he may say something out loud while being totally oblivious to what is going on around him. It appears that the child is talking in an impulsive manner, but actually the child is unaware of his effect on others. Kevin regularly showed signs of impulsivity when his routine was interrupted, similar to PDD children. However, he also sought out other children to "annoy" with his belching and jokes. His seeking out others is more typical of ADHD.

The key to differentiating between PDD and ADHD is often the severity of the social problems. The social problems Kevin exhibited were more profound than found in ADHD. In kindergarten, Kevin was totally disinterested in peers. He engaged in solitary play. By junior high, he was engaged with a few other children around specific interests such as Pokémon cards. It was a hopeful sign when he began to curtail his teasing of girls and actually began to develop more positive relationships with a couple of them. Most PDD children have few, if any, friends. ADHD children, by contrast, generally seek out others. They are interested in making friends, but they sometimes lack social skills, such as listening or thinking about what to say before saying it.

Though children usually have one diagnosis or the other, there are some PDD children who like Kevin also show ADHD-like behavior. Kevin would often be distracted by what other children were doing in the classroom, and this is characteristic of ADHD. In addition, Kevin also interrupted others and had trouble waiting his turn, which is also seen in ADHD children.

DSM-IV indicates that children can have either ADHD or PDD, but not both. *DSM-IV* mentions that a PDD child may show some signs of hyperactivity, but not always. However, it is important to differentiate the group of PDD children who have ADHD-like symptoms from those children who do not. Treatment is different for those PDD children who also have ADHD-like symptoms. A number of recent studies suggest there are two types of PDD children, those with ADHD-like symptoms, such as hyperactivity, and those without these problems. One study indicates that the PDD group with ADHD on average has more serious difficulties, such as more severe agitation and aggressive outbursts sometimes requiring hospital visits and additional medications. Furthermore, the same study shows that the PDD group with ADHD truly has symptoms of both disorders. Another study shows that medication for ADHD helps reduce the hyper-active symptoms of autistic children but not social problems or preoccupations. This study supports the idea that separate treat-ments are useful for each set of problems.

We shall consider the mixed group a case of dual diagnosis, though it is more in keeping with *DSM-IV* to consider it a sub-group within the PDD category. It makes sense to separate out these dual-diagnosis cases, as the treatment and prognosis is often different. Unfortunately many doctors do not consider that these problems can occur together, so they treat one disorder or the other, not both. Kevin is an example of this dual-diagnosis issue. Early on one psychiatrist diagnosed him with ADHD, while another psychiatrist who saw Kevin some years later decided he had PDD-NOS. However, in reality he had some symptoms of both disorders, and he did better when both were recognized.

Psychological Treatment of ADHD and PDD

If your child has both disorders, the treatment approach should take both into account. The behavior-modification strategies and medications that are typically used for ADHD alone must be modified when the child also has PDD. The goals of a behavior-modification program need to be simpler, and improvement will be even more gradual in dual-diagnosis cases. With Kevin, we started with the basic goals of learning not to hit or spit, and it took several months to be successful. Goals like completing assign-ments must wait until the more pressing self-control issues are addressed.

You are also going to have to be more directly involved in many tasks, such as getting your child ready for school in the morning. A child with this dual diagnosis is harder to motivate because there is greater distractibility and often a lack of interest in self-care tasks. Rather than give your child an incentive to get dressed, you will probably need to assist. The teacher will also need to assist your child with assignments in class. Often an aide or a smaller special education class will be necessary.

An important feature of therapy with PDD children, namely the focus on social development, needs to be integrated into the therapy for dual-diagnosis children. Focusing on social interaction is critical, and this often involves some individual therapy at the start rather than a social-skills training group. The child with PDD is generally too socially immature to know how to relate with a group of children. The therapist meets individually with your child to find out how to build a bond with him. Then the therapist coaches you on how to join the child in some favorite activity outside the sessions. In the case of Kevin, we did this and discovered an activity and a style of interaction that Kevin enjoyed and then coached his parents to form this kind of bond at home. A year later, Kevin was interested in social interaction with peers, and we gradually encouraged and planned one-on-one peer interactions on the weekends. Kevin's parents helped him seek out a peer who had similar interests, and the get-togethers began with short meetings at Kevin's house. Eventually, Kevin began to seek out this child on his own. Kevin was also encouraged to begin riding horses, which became a family activity. He took private lessons. Generally, it is not recommended that group activities with peers be pushed early on because dealing with several children at once can be difficult for a PDD child.

One other strategy that has been helpful for some children with dual diagnoses is a cognitive behavioral approach to cope with frustration. Changes in routine are difficult for these children. The parent or teacher uses a short catchphrase whenever a change in routine is about to occur. This cue helps the child anticipate and cope with change. One example is the phrase "we'll play that again soon." This phrase reminds the child that stopping an activity is not forever. Catchphrases usually take months to become effective in helping the dual-diagnosis child deal with frustrations. One way to jump-start the process is to use strong rewards early on for signs of flexibility. Eventually, tantrums and other forms of resistance diminish, and acceptance of change is easier.

With autism, which is a more severe form of PDD than what Kevin exhibited, the goals are more basic and progress is even slower. Special education is a must with these children. They often have severely limited communication skills, and many are not able to carry on a conversation at all. The goals of language development and communication skills take precedence over social interaction skills.

Medication Management

It is important to consult with a psychiatrist who is familiar with both disorders to decide what kind of medication to use. Stimulant medication often helps control ADHD symptoms like distractibility, hyperactivity, and impulsivity. For PDD, treatment is often "problem focused." If your child exhibits a recurring symptom, such as obsessive behavior or anxious thoughts, then a medication is selected for this problem.

Few controlled studies have been done for the pharmacological treatment of autistic spectrum disorders. The FDA has not approved any medications for the treatment of autistic disorders. However, medications can be effective in treating some of the symptoms such as obsessive thoughts, compulsive behaviors, irritability, aggression, hyperactivity, attentional problems, anxiety, and depression. Medications used for the treatment of the autistic spectrum disorders include stimulants, serotonin reuptake inhibitors, alpha 2 adrenergics, typical antipsychotics, atypical antipsychotics, and mood stabilizers.

If your child is more anxious or has low mood, an antidepressant may be tried. The SSRIs (see Table 6.1) are used for treatment of depressive and anxiety symptoms in children and adolescents who have PDD. The serotonin reuptake inhibitors have also sometimes been effective for the treatment of preoccupations and rigid adherence to routines.

If your child is preoccupied by internal thoughts or is excessively hostile and agitated, then a trial of an antipsychotic may be tried. Recent drug studies support the use of *atypical* antipsychotics. In particular, risperidone was shown to be effective for the reduction of aggression and repetitive behavior. In addition, in some children there was an increase in positive interactions with others. Generally, atypical antipsychotics (see Table 6.3) also may be used for mood swings, chronic agitation, obsessions, hyperactivity, and impulsivity.

The *typical* antipsychotics, such as haloperidol (Haldol), thioridazine (Mellaril), and chlorpromazine (Thorazine), have also been used, but they have a higher risk of side effects, such as tardive dyskinesia (involuntary movements of the tongue, neck, or body). There has been more research on the effectiveness of the typical antipsychotics, as they have been available for many years. These medications can help reduce stereotypical behavior, repetitive speech, interpersonal withdrawal, and fidgetiness. Because of the higher risk of side effects of the typical antipsychotics, psychiatrists nowadays generally prefer using the atypicals.

Much more rarely, the mood stabilizers (see Table 6.4) are used for treatment of continuous fluctuations of mood that do not respond to treatment with atypical antipsychotics or antidepressants.

Finally, studies of clonidine, which activates adrenergic brain receptors, show a reduction of impulsivity, hyperactivity, and irritability for the first few months of treatment, but tolerance to clonidine develops several months later. The drug becomes ineffective when it is used for these problems over a prolonged period.

Interestingly, some studies show that medications used for ADHD also help symptoms of PDD while other studies indicate that stimulants can bring about irritability, preoccupations, and tics in some PDD children. If these medications are tried for your child's PDD, you and the doctors should evaluate whether the child's PDD symptoms are affected positively or negatively. It is more likely that ADHD symptoms like hyperactivity or distractibility will be improved, rather than PDD symptoms, such as rigid adherence to routines.

On rare occasions, a psychiatrist may determine that a child originally diagnosed as having PDD and ADHD manifests signs of psychotic thinking instead. If a child shows any psychotic symptoms, such as delusions, hallucinations, or disorganized speech, we would not recommend using the ADHD medications, particularly one of the stimulants. Stimulant medication will, in many cases, increase psychotic symptoms. Any psychotic symptoms should be treated first with antipsychotic medication, and then your child should be evaluated to determine if other problems are present.

When treating children with symptoms of PDD and ADHD, the psychiatrist must determine which symptoms are more prominent and should be treated first. Also, the doctor must monitor potential side effects. For example, sometimes too much of a stimulant can cause children with PDD- and ADHD-like symptoms to become irritable or withdrawn. This was the case for Kevin, so that stimulant medication was discontinued. The doctor in Kevin's case also felt that the PDD symptoms did not require medication: his anger was controlled with behavior modification, and his mood was generally good.

If medications are used, the dosage of antipsychotics or antidepressants can often be lowered, or sometimes discontinued, after the child has been stable for an extended period of time, usually six months or more. ADHD medications are often continued longer, depending on their usefulness.

When Tics Are Part of the Picture

What should parents do if their child with ADHD develops a tic disorder? A related question is whether stimulant medication has something to do with the emergence of tics. First, let us define tics. The *DSM-IV* defines a tic as "a sudden, rapid, recurrent, nonrhythmic, stereotyped motor movement or vocalization." In other words, a tic can be a repeated limb movement, like shoulder shrugging, or a tic can be expressed by a facial gesture, such as eye blinking or grimacing. The tics are not intended by the child and appear out of place. Another possibility is a vocal tic, such as a grunting noise or throat clearing. The child can often suppress tics for a short time. However, this requires continuous effort on the child's part, and generally when the child relaxes the tics return. They usually occur many times a day, but not every day. If they occur over at least a four-week period, then they are diagnosed as a tic disorder.

One type of tic disorder that children sometimes exhibit is called Tourette's disorder. To be called Tourette's, there need to be both motor and vocal tics for a period of at least a year (*DSM-IV*). The symptoms generally begin in childhood or early adolescence and often diminish or disappear in adulthood. Tourette's is a genetic disorder that usually can be effectively treated by medication.

Epidemiological and clinical studies differ on the rates of ADHD seen among individuals with Tourette's disorder. Some studies report rates as high as 50 percent of children with Tourette's disorder also have ADHD. Tourette's disorder is relatively rare, though, occurring in about one in two thousand people (*DSM-IV*). Thus, the number of children with both disorders is also rare.

Animal models and clinical studies in humans have led to the hypothesis that the tics of Tourette's disorder are owing to excess dopamine or an increased sensitivity of D2 dopamine receptors. Dopamine is a neurotransmitter in the brain. Clinical trials support this dopaminergic mechanism of action, and antipsychotic medications that block dopaminergic D2 receptors have been effective in suppressing tics.

Larry: Psychotherapy Helps with Tourette's and ADHD

Larry, a sixth-grade boy, had been diagnosed with Tourette's and ADHD and was taking a small dose of risperidone, an atypical antipsychotic, for his tics, but he continued to show ADHD symptoms. Larry had difficulty staying on task in class, his backpack and folders were a mess, and he talked in class without permission. In addition, at home he argued about chores. On the other hand, the medication had mostly controlled his tics. Before starting medication, he blinked his eyes in an exaggerated way, made facial grimaces at times, and often jerked his arms and neck. These motor tics were significantly less since he was put on medication. Furthermore, he previously exhibited vocal tics—clearing of the throat and making screeching sounds. These had stopped entirely on medicine.

Unfortunately, Larry had not tolerated a stimulant for the ADHD symptoms: his tics had worsened and the medication was discontinued. He also tried a nonstimulant, bupropion, but there was no effect on the ADHD symptoms, so his doctor settled on the risperidone for his tics. Because ADHD medication was no longer an option, a behavior-modification strategy at home was implemented to help with homework and chores. Fun activities, like playing his video game system, became contingent on a daily basis with his chores and homework being completed. This strategy worked well, except when Larry's mother made additional requests (beyond homework and regular chores). Then, Larry would argue with her. Larry's mother was asked by the therapist to write these additional requests on index cards. Each day his mom would put certain cards out on the dining room table, and Larry would check them after school. In this way, the arguments were avoided, and he became more cooperative. Part of the success may have come from avoiding verbal discussion of chores. Another factor may have been that Larry felt more in control because the cards were a predictable part of his routine after school. Larry could check the cards and know right away what extra chores he had to do that day. There were no surprises.

Another strategy that helped lessen arguing was use of a calming "mantra." Larry was asked to say a calming phrase to himself when adults made a request. The phrase he liked to use was "let it go" ("it" referred to his anger). He practiced saying this to himself several times a day and was eventually able to calm himself with it.

In school, Larry felt teased and ostracized at times, which he attributed to the tics. When we looked more closely at the times he was teased, the tics didn't seem to be the reason; there seemed to be a different cause. He would usually be criticized when he would not listen to peers' suggestions—a social skills deficit that sometimes occurs with ADHD. We practiced more appropriate ways of responding to peers, and the feelings of rejection lessened considerably.

In addition, we talked about telling one of his friends about his tics. By practicing in our sessions how to explain tics to a friend, Larry got a clearer idea himself about what tics and Tourette's were and what caused them. When he was ready, he explained to a friend at school that his body makes jerking movements sometimes, and that he couldn't help it. The other boy listened and continued to be friendly, which made Larry feel more comfortable about his tics. Another factor that helped him to become more comfortable was our explanation to Larry that tics often lessen later in adolescence.

Another idea that we did not use in this case is to have the teacher read a story about Tourette's to the class. The students would come to understand Tourette's and would be more accepting of a classmate's tics. This strategy would be especially suitable for classmates of a younger child.

Research into Tics, ADHD, and Stimulant Medications

Individuals with both ADHD and Tourette's disorder are at significant risk for poor outcomes owing to social difficulties. These children often are teased by other children and sometimes are viewed as more aggressive, less likeable, and more withdrawn than their peers. Studies have shown that children who have both ADHD and Tourette's disorder are also at high risk for mood disorders, anxiety, oppositional defiant disorder, and conduct disorder.

Several researchers have shown that most of the problems these children have in school are owing to ADHD, not Tourette's disorder. One study, which looked at children with both Tourette's and ADHD, concluded it was the onset of ADHD that worsened children's behavior problems. Children with Tourette's alone did not show behavior problems at home or school, though they did exhibit some social withdrawal and anxiety about how others would react to their tics. It is the ADHD symptoms, not tics, that can affect academic performance and behavior.

When tics develop, they usually begin about two and a half years after ADHD symptoms have been observed. In one study, about a third of children with ADHD had tics as well. Some of these children were already receiving stimulant medication. In another study, a smaller sample of ADHD children who had not begun medication was surveyed, and again about a third had some form of tics. Thus, tics can also occur in ADHD children where there is no stimulant medication.

For ADHD children with tic disorders, some studies suggest that stimulants are effective. However, what the studies mean by effective is that ADHD behaviors are reduced, but tics are not. The good news is that tics did not worsen in these studies; the bad news is that they did not improve with the stimulant medication.

What should parents do if tics persist or get worse with stimulant treatment of ADHD? Sometimes tics worsen, especially at higher doses of stimulant medication. In these cases, stimulants are usually stopped. The problem then is that ADHD symptoms recur and can be difficult to manage. Also, the tics often do not go away once stimulant medication is discontinued. What else can be tried in these cases?

Alternate Medications for ADHD and Tics

If ADHD medications are needed to treat the ADHD symptoms, but tics persist or worsen, one alternative is to add a medication that helps control the tics. The noradrenergic medications clonidine and guanfacine are two medications that are being used effectively in many cases. Some studies indicate that clonidine or guanfacine work well alone, and others indicate that a small dose of stimulant medication needs to be added in order to improve the ADHD symptoms.

Another possibility is to add an antipsychotic medication instead of one of the noradrenergics. Antipsychotic medications that block the D2 dopaminergic receptors have been effective in several double-blind clinical trials for the suppression of tics in Tourette's disorder. These medications include haloperidol, pimozide, tiapride, fluphenazine, and others. Haloperidol and pimozide have been studied more than the other antipsychotics for the treatment of tics.

The atypical antipsychotics are beginning to be used in place of haloperidol and pimozide because the risk of side effects such as tardive dyskinesia (involuntary movements of the tongue, head, or body) appears to be lower. The atypical antipsychotics that have been studied the most are risperidone and ziprasidone, as they block dopaminergic D2 receptors better than the other atypicals do. Double-blind placebo-controlled trials of risperidone and ziprasidone have shown a 32 to 35 percent decrease in tic symptoms with few side effects. Often stimulant medication is used in conjunction with the antipsychotic medication in order to help control the ADHD symptoms.

Another class of medications that is sometimes helpful in dual-diagnosis cases is the tricyclics—namely, imipramine and desipramine. These medications in the past were the primary treatment for depressive disorders. Currently, they are sometimes used in the treatment of ADHD with tics. In these cases, ADHD medications are not used. However, the tricyclics, as well as the noradrenergic medicines, have potential cardiovascular side effects, so it is important to talk this over with your doctor and monitor your child's symptoms. Electrocardiogram monitoring is essential before starting either of these medications owing to the risk, though rare, of sudden death. A repeat electrocardiogram should be done after each dose increase and yearly thereafter.

CHAPTER 9

ADHD and Other Issues

Sleep Disorders and Substance Abuse

ADHD children and adolescents may exhibit other problems, such as sleep difficulties, and many parents ask if these problems are related to ADHD. They also want to know what they can do to help their ADHD child get a good night's rest. Some parents of older children and adolescents have concerns about their adolescents' use of cigarettes, or other substances like alcohol, marijuana, and harder drugs. In this chapter, we will review current research about these problems as well as make practical suggestions for you.

Charles: His Motor Won't Stop at Bedtime

Charles's parents reported that he was always "on the go." He would not slow up at night. They would try reading him a story or talking quietly in bed, but he still got out of bed after his parents left his room. He would either play in his room or wander around the house in search of something to do. He had a younger brother who slept in the room with him, and frequently those noises would wake up his brother. His parents became extremely frustrated, because they had to put both boys to bed all over again. Charles took stimulant medication during the day for his ADHD symptoms. The doctor tried reducing the medication to see if that would help Charles wind down at night, but to no avail. The only strategy that his parents found helped Charles to go to sleep was for his father to lie down in bed with him. His father had to stay until Charles fell asleep, which would take a half hour or so. Many times his father fell asleep during this time, and Charles's mother ended up coming in to wake up her husband!

His parents tried putting the younger brother to sleep in a different room, so that they could let Charles stay up later to play with toys in his room. Their hope was that he would eventually get tired and go to sleep when he was ready. However, now Charles would stay up close to midnight. His father ended up having to lie down in bed with him, just as before. They were back to the same problem, only now it was much later in the evening!

Medications That Can Help Sleep Disorders

A number of children with ADHD have trouble falling asleep at night. The problem can take several forms. Like Charles, they may not want to lie down in bed. Other ADHD children thrash about under their covers; some take an hour or more to fall asleep; some awaken frequently in the middle of the night; while some have trouble awakening in the morning. Your child may exhibit one or more of these problems. Research indicates that between 20 and 50 percent of ADHD children have sleep problems.

The risk increases for children taking stimulant medication. In some cases, medication given later in the day may need to be reduced. If a long-acting dose is being prescribed, it may need to be changed to a short-acting form. Parents and doctors will need to adjust the amount and timing of the stimulant medication in order to find out what works best for each child.

Another possibility is to change to a nonstimulant medication as the primary treatment for ADHD. Nonstimulant medications are less likely to interfere with sleep. An example would be the medicine atomoxetine (Strattera). The problem is that this means making a major change in your child's treatment regimen. If the stimulant medications were working well during the daytime to reduce distractibility and impulsivity, you may be reluctant to change the treatment.

Another choice is to keep your child on stimulant medication during the day but add a secondary medication for sleep. This is what worked for Charles. One possible medication is an antihistamine medication called diphenhydramine. In the central nervous system, diphenhydramine blocks the histamine H1 receptor thereby causing sleepiness. Diphenhydramine usually works for only a few weeks if given on consecutive nights, because most people develop tolerance to it after one week. Some people react adversely to diphenhydramine and experience anxiety, restlessness, and insomnia; if there are these side effects, it should be discontinued. The recommended dosage is 12.5 to 50 mg given at bedtime.

An alternative medication for short-term treatment of insomnia is zolpidem (Ambien). This nonbenzodiazepine sedative hypnotic has a strong sedating effect. Possible side effects include headache, dizziness, lightheadedness, and nausea. In a small study of only twelve children ages eight to thirteen, the single adverse event was in one patient who reported dizziness. Treatment should be limited to two consecutive weeks or to intermittent use at the lowest effective dose. If the medication is continued nightly for many weeks, people may develop tolerance to the medication. The dosage options are 5 mg or 10 mg tablets at bedtime.

Another nonbenzodiazepine sedative hypnotic for short-term treatment of insomnia is zaleplon (Sonata). Side effects are similar to zolpidem (Ambien). The major difference between zolpidem and zaleplon is that zaleplon is absorbed and eliminated more quickly and thus has a shorter effect than zolpidem. Sometimes parents and doctors want a shorter-acting sleep medication, particularly if the child wakes up feeling sleepy in the mornings. In that case, zaleplon is usually preferred. Another option to prevent morning sleepiness is to give either of these medications a little earlier in the evening so that its effect will be gone by morning. The dosage for zaleplon is 5 to 20 mg at bedtime, and it is available in 5 mg and 10 mg capsules.

A medication used frequently for long-term treatment of insomnia is trazadone. This medication is an old antidepressant that is used in low doses from 25 mg to 100 mg for the treatment of insomnia in children and adults. If a child needs help with sleep for more than a few weeks, this medication is preferable because people do not develop a tolerance on trazadone.

Eszopiclone (Lunesta), a new medication for sleep, was approved by the FDA in 2005 for long-term use by adults. Studies involving children may be forthcoming. As with all medications, it is imperative to have a physician closely monitor the use of these medications in your child.

Psychological Sleep Strategies

Parents can try using sleep strategies with their child before altering the child's medications. There are different strategies possible, depending on whether the problem occurs getting to sleep, awakening at night, or staying in bed past morning.

Getting to Sleep

It is useful to practice certain rituals before bedtime to help children become relaxed and ready for sleep. First, a "wind down" time is suggested. Rather than play intense video games right up until bedtime, start moving your child toward quieter activities about an hour before bed. For young children, one example would be reading a story together, or talking about the day in bed. Sometimes parents sit next to their child in bed; however, if your child has trouble separating from you at night, it would be advisable for you to sit in a chair rather than in your child's bed. Otherwise, you may find your child crying or protesting and getting revved up again, when you get out of his bed. Usually you will want to complete all other bedtime activities, such as bathing or teeth brushing, before you do the wind-down activity. If your child gets back up, you may have trouble getting him to settle down again in bed.

Another helpful bedtime ritual is to have your child go to bed around the same time each night. Our bodies operate on a circadian rhythm; in other words, our body's chemicals and our sleep-wake cycle operate on a twenty-four hour cycle for the most part. If a child goes to bed around the same time, his body will more likely adjust to that sleep cycle.

Nighttime Awakening

Studies that measure movements throughout the night show that ADHD children tend to move about in bed more than average. Do not become concerned if you find the covers on the floor in the morning. Just as some ADHD children move their hands or legs a lot during the day, they may do the same at night. It is only a problem if moving about at night interrupts your child's sleep frequently. One study suggests that generally these upper and lower limb movements do not disturb children's sleep.

However, if your child does often awaken during the night and comes to talk to you, we would recommend that you keep your contact brief and try to have the child return to his bed to sleep. If your child falls asleep in your bed, this will become such a "treat" for your child that it will likely happen on many more occasions. When your child returns to his own bed, have him lie down. If necessary, turn on some soft music or have him look at a book or magazine for a short time. Do not insist that your child lay still and sleep. Sleep will more likely occur if your child is relaxed and lying down, but not necessarily "trying" to sleep.

Over time, the goal would be for your child to use these calming strategies by himself, without having to disturb you.

Difficulty Waking in the Morning

When it is time to wake up in the morning, some parents have trouble getting their ADHD child up. Some children, even if they do not have a restless night, will be in a deep sleep in the morning. No matter how tired they are, it is important to wake up your child on time anyway. Use a loud alarm and open all the shades in the room. Later in the day, if your child acts tired, try to prevent him from napping. Napping in the afternoon will make it more difficult for your child to sleep well during the night.

ADHD children tend to be unfocused in the morning and tend to daydream, rather than get ready for school. One strategy is to give your child his stimulant medication as soon as possible; within an hour it should help him to be more attentive. However, many times the child needs to be ready to leave the house in less than an hour, before the medicine starts working. In that case, an early morning schedule with incentives may help. Making it a routine will help the child to get in the habit of doing what is necessary before leaving home. The incentive could be some brief activity that your child enjoys. For some children, this may be a cartoon or using their hand-held game system if they get up and get ready in time. It should come last in the morning ritual, so that the child has an added reason to get ready as soon as possible. It is important to make sure this activity does not begin until the child is completely ready for school, or you will have a hard time getting him to do any other morning chores. One last suggestion if all else fails: some doctors recommend waking the child up forty-five minutes early, giving him his morning medicine, and then telling him to lie back down to rest or sleep. The idea is that when it is really time to wake up, the child will have the benefit of his medication to help him.

A number of research studies indicate that there may be another problem besides ADHD that is affecting the sleep of these children. Possible secondary problems that can interfere with sleep are oppositionality, depression, or anxiety. If your child continues to have difficulties sleeping, have a psychologist evaluate whether he has one of the co-occurring conditions that we've looked at in earlier chapters. Once any secondary problems are treated, your child's sleep is likely to improve.

Tom and Ned: Teens Who Smoke and Drink

Tom and Ned were two of the teens we discussed in Chapter 7. In addition to violating rules in their home or school, these boys were daily smokers. Ned began in junior high, and Tom began in high school. They were exposed to cigarettes by their friends, and Ned also had two parents who smoked. Both teenagers talked about feeling calmer when they smoked, and both felt they would be able to stop someday. Despite knowing how addictive and harmful cigarettes could be, the teenagers felt invulnerable.

Interestingly, both boys had a behavior disorder in addition to ADHD. Each of these diagnoses alone is a risk factor for smoking. ADHD is a risk factor because nicotine has a temporary calming effect on the symptoms of distractibility and impulsivity. One theory about why behavior disorders are a risk factor is that these teens tend to reject adult rules and suggestions even more than other teens. Unless their friends frown on smoking, these teens will not usually be motivated to stop. In college, some of Tom's friends smoked and some did not. During his sophomore year, he became attached to a girlfriend who encouraged him to stop, and he started working on it.

Both these teenagers also drank alcohol and smoked pot on weekends and sometimes during the week. Again, they did this with their friends, not alone. Ned had a bigger problem drinking to excess than Tom. He would get drunk frequently on the weekends and sometimes smoked pot before school. He cared less than Tom about his academic performance and did not go on to college after high school. Ned had the more serious diagnosis of conduct disorder, so that he had little or no qualms about violating society's rules about drugs. Tom was oppositional, but he still did not want to get in serious trouble with the police or his parents.

Research on Cigarette Use

Smoking, drinking, and other substance abuse can be a problem among some adolescents with ADHD. Smoking cigarettes regularly was reported in about 50 percent of teens with ADHD, about twice as many as age-mates without ADHD. Another study found that 30 percent of ADHD teens smoked daily, more than double the number of teens without ADHD. These statistics are worrisome to parents of ADHD children. Why are cigarettes such a problem for ADHD teens? What can be done to lessen the chance that your child will some day turn to smoking?

Cigarettes contain nicotine, which is a stimulant, and scientists think that this makes cigarettes especially appealing to ADHD youth. It can have a settling effect, though temporary, on ADHD symptoms of distractibility and impulsivity. There are also studies that show nicotine's positive effect on cognitive performance and attention in teens with ADHD.

Another factor leading to cigarette use among ADHD teens is that they often choose friends who smoke. Before your child takes up smoking, keep an eye on his friends. If possible, limit his contact with others who smoke. Of course, if one of the adults in your household smokes, this will also increase the chances of your child trying cigarettes. Once an ADHD child tries smoking, it is likely to be quite rewarding, owing to the nicotine, and it is likely to continue. Thus, parents ought to do what they can to limit exposure to cigarettes before smoking becomes a problem. We strongly recommend that parents try to quit smoking and forbid any smoking in their house.

As we saw before with Tom and Ned, many ADHD teens who smoke have a dual diagnosis with a behavior disorder. Studies have confirmed that there is an increased risk of smoking if teens have a conduct disorder. ADHD is one risk factor, and conduct disorder is another. Thus, if your child is diagnosed with a conduct disorder as well as ADHD, it is even more likely that he will turn to cigarettes.

Because the dual diagnosis of ADHD and conduct disorder is a "red flag" for potential addiction to cigarettes, it would be especially important for parents to talk about cigarette use and its dangers with children who show the beginning signs of both these disorders. If your child shows some signs of a conduct disorder, greater supervision of peer activities at a young age is critical to limit, if possible, your child's exposure to other teens who smoke. You will not always be able to prevent your child's exposure to smokers, but one approach would be to increase his involvement in structured activities, like sports or scouts, where smoking is less likely to occur.

Research on Drug Use

While "abuse" of other substances does not seem significantly related to ADHD in teenagers, some studies of "use," as opposed to "abuse," have shown that ADHD is a factor. By "use" the researchers mean any experimentation with drugs, and by "abuse" they mean consistent use over a period of a year, such that there develops impairment in the person's functioning at school, work, or home. The percentage of teens that abuse drugs is estimated at between 15 to 30 percent. These statistics were the same whether or not the teens had ADHD. Interestingly, it is the diagnosis of conduct disorder, not ADHD, that predicts drug abuse in adolescence.

There is a somewhat increased chance of experimentation with alcohol and drugs by ADHD youth, however. A recent study indicates that ADHD leads to a greater number of alcohol-related problems, though not a full-fledged alcohol abuse disorder. In other words, adolescents with ADHD are more likely to experiment and may occasionally go overboard. Specifically, there were more episodes of drunkenness reported in this recent study.

What is especially worrisome is that experimentation during the teenage years may lead to abuse as an adult. We do not know for sure if those ADHD teens who experiment with drugs will become addicted by adulthood. However, we do know that drug abuse is a serious problem for *adults* with ADHD. The percent of drug abuse rises dramatically for ADHD adults. Recent research shows that drug abuse rises from 15 percent among ADHD youth to about 50 percent in adults with ADHD. This is twice that for adults without ADHD. Several questions come to mind about these statistics for substance abuse. Why do many more adults with ADHD abuse substances? Is ADHD the causative factor? Further, is the use of stimulant medication by children and adolescents a risk for drug abuse during adolescence or adulthood?

There are no research reports on why the abuse becomes greater in numbers in adulthood. It is possible that parental supervision and high school attendance lessen drug abuse by teens. When they become adults, there is less supervision and structure. In addition, there are increasing stresses in adulthood, for example, the stress to become financially independent. The abuse of drugs may increase in response to the pressures of adult life and the lack of supervision.

Those adults with ADHD who also have bipolar disorder have an even greater risk of substance abuse. As we saw in Chapter 2, with bipolar disorder there is a significant disturbance in regulation of emotions. People who have bipolar disorder experience a lot of ups and downs. Many of these adults may turn to substances to try to control unpleasant, and often painful, fluctuations in their moods.

Stimulant Medication and Other Treatment Issues

An important finding in the last few years is that one of the main ways to limit the effect of ADHD on later substance abuse is the use of stimulant medication during childhood. There are a number of studies showing that stimulant treatment does not increase substance abuse, and that it actually reduces the risk for substance abuse later in life. It seems that the more ADHD is controlled by medication, the less likely the adult will turn to dangerous drugs to try to regulate ADHD-related problems.

If your teen does develop a substance-abuse problem, it is important to treat the substance abuse first and then to reassess to determine whether ADHD remains a problem. Consult with a substance-abuse specialist in your area to determine whether inpatient or day treatment may be needed. In either case, it will be important to find out how drugs have become available to your teen, so you can limit his exposure to those who have made the drugs available. This often means preventing your teen from hanging out with the same friends. It may be difficult to do this without sending your teen away to the hospital or to a structured boarding school. It is difficult to enforce rules about whom your teen sees, because parents cannot follow teens around. One suggestion would be to involve your teen in a rehab group or an Alcoholics Anonymous group that meets many times a week. Besides learning about his addiction, your teen will be exposed to other teens who are trying to remain sober. Hopefully, new and healthier friendships will be formed.

Psychotherapy may also be helpful for children and adolescents with ADHD and substance-abuse problems. Psychotherapy should focus on the abuse problems. The therapist should talk with your teen about the purpose that alcohol or illegal drugs serve in his life. The therapist would then help support more positive ways of dealing with the teen's problems. It is also important for the therapist to support your teen's participation in group programs with other teens. In this way, the teen's thinking about his problems as well as his peer group might change.

The psychopharmacological treatment of ADHD in adolescents who abuse substances is difficult owing to poor compliance—it is very difficult to get ADHD teens with substance-abuse problems to reliably take their medicine. They have been used to taking drugs when they want to get "high," whereas the prescribed medications will not make them "high," just help maintain an even mood and reduce distractibility. Another problem is that there needs to be a period of abstinence of two to four weeks before beginning pharmacological treatment. If your teen does not stop using abused substances first, it is unlikely medications will work. There could even be dangerous interactions between the medications and the abused drugs. Antidepressants should be tried before stimulants for teens with substance abuse and ADHD, as there is a potential for abuse with stimulants. Bupropion (Wellbutrin XL), a medication with no known abuse potential, can help reduce ADHD symptoms as well as help reduce substance-craving symptoms. Wellbutrin XL is the longest-acting form of bupropion and is dosed initially at 150 mg every morning, with the potential to increase to 300 mg every morning after one month on 150 mg. Another choice for treatment is one of the tricyclic antidepressant medications, because they also have low abuse potential and may help with ADHD. A couple of studies done with adults indicate that medications like bupropion and tricyclic antidepressants have had a moderate effect on substance abuse and ADHD.

If Wellbutrin XL and the tricyclic antidepressants are ineffective, or cause side effects, then stimulants should be initiated. When there is a history of substance abuse, stimulant treatment of ADHD should be limited to the long-acting preparations such as Concerta, Ritalin LA, or Adderall XR owing to their lower likelihood of being abused compared to the short-acting prescriptions. Because amphetamines, like Adderall, have a greater euphoric effect than methylphenidate products, like Concerta, Metadate CD, or Ritalin LA, the first line of treatment is usually one of the methylphenidate products. If side effects occur on the long-acting preparations, then one of the medium-acting preparations should be considered.

Final Thoughts

Where Do You Go from Here?

We hope you have learned about the various diagnoses that can be affecting your child in addition to ADHD. In more than half of cases, there is an additional psychological problem that needs to be addressed in order for your child to be successful in the social and academic areas of his life.

You can try to implement some of our suggestions at home and in school. In Chapters 1, 3, and 5, we designed educational approaches for children who have ADHD by itself or in conjunction with a mood disorder. You might discuss the ideas with your child's teacher, and try to reach a common game plan together. You also might want to consult with an educational therapist who can teach your child effective learning techniques and can consult with you and you child's teacher.

Throughout the book, we made a number of other suggestions for helping develop social skills, self-esteem, and self-control for children with different diagnoses. Think about which of these ideas will work best for your child. Also, think carefully about which dual diagnosis fits your child's problems. Which therapeutic approaches make the most sense for your child? You may want to review your thoughts with a child psychologist or psychiatrist. Does a professional outside observer agree with your hunches about your child?

A child psychologist or psychiatrist can tell you if your child's problems are actually signs of a significant dual diagnosis that requires psychological or medical attention. I remember when I was in graduate school and the professors talked about "medical student's disease." This so-called disease occurs when the reader of a medical or psychiatric text sees his own idiosyncrasies as signs of a serious illness. This can happen to the reader of this book as well. No psychological diagnosis is so foreign that you or your child may not experience some of the symptoms. But to apply to your child, the problems must be pervasive and disruptive. By "pervasive," we mean that the problems occur in various situations over many months. By "disruptive," we mean that the problems interfere with the child's daily functioning in school or at home.

Many of these dual diagnoses will require outside help to be treated effectively. Ask your friends, teachers, or local support groups, such as Children and Adults with Attention-Deficit/ Hyperactivity Disorder (CHADD; a group for parents whose children have ADHD), where they have found help. Ask for someone who has worked with children, not just adults, and then share with that professional your ideas after reading this book. Make sure you feel comfortable that the clinician wants to work together with you, the parents, and your child. Treating ADHD and dual diagnoses is a team effort that requires the coordination of professionals, parents, and teachers. If the doctor has no interest in working with you or the teachers, think about finding another doctor. Not every doctor is familiar with the challenges of treating ADHD children with dual diagnoses.

If you want to read more in a particular area, we have provided you with references, organized by chapter, at the end of this book. Many of the articles and books we reference are written for professionals, rather than parents, and there may be some terms you do not understand. However, you will comprehend the major points, and you may be able to ask questions about the medical terms if you have a friend with some medical training. Another possibility is to make a copy of the article for your doctor, and ask him or her to spend a few minutes with you answering your questions. Another suggestion would be to do a search for the medical terms on the Internet, where you may get some useful explanations.

Keep asking questions because the more you learn, the better you will know what to do to help your child. You are your child's best advocate, and we hope this book will empower you to get your child the best help available in your community.

References

Preface

Diagnostic and Statistical Manual of Mental Disorders. 4th ed. (Washington, D.C.: American Psychiatric Association, 1994.)

Goldman, Larry; Gentel, Myron; and Besman, Rebecca. Diagnosis and treatment of attention–deficit/hyperactivity disorder in children and adolescents. *Journal of American Medical Association*. 279 (1998): 1100–7.

Jensen, Peter; Hinshaw, Stephen; Kraemer, Helena; Lenora, Nilantha; Newcorn, Jeffrey; Abikoff, Howard; March, John; Arnold, Eugene; Cantwell, Dennis; Conners, C. Keith; Elliott, Glen; Greenhill, Laurence; Hechtman, Lily; Hoza, Betsy; Pelham, William; Severe, Joanne; Swanson, James; Wells, Karen; Wigal, Timothy; and Vitiello, Benedetto. ADHD comorbidity findings from the MTA study: comparing comorbid subgroups. *Journal of American Academy of Child and Adolescent Psychiatry*. 40 (2001): 147–58.

Jensen, Peter; Martin, David; and Cantwell, Dennis. Comorbidity in ADHD: implications for research, practice, and DSM-V. *Journal of American Academy of Child and Adolescent Psychiatry*. 36 (1997): 1065–80.

Newcorn, Jeffrey; Halperin, Jeffrey; Jensen, Peter; Abikoff, Howard; Arnold, Eugene; Cantwell, Dennis; Conners, C. Keith; Elliott, Glen; Epstein, Jeffrey; Greenhill, Laurence; Hechtman, Lily; Hinshaw, Stephen; Hoza, Betsy; Kraemer, Helena; Pelham, William; Severe, Joanne; Swanson, James;

Wells, Karen; Wigal, Timothy; and Vitiello, Benedetto. Symptom profiles in children with ADHD: effects of comorbidity and gender. *Journal of American Academy of Child and Adolescent Psychiatry*. 40 (2001): 137–46.

Chapter 1

Barkley, Russell. Attention-deficit/hyperactivity disorder. *Scientific American*. 279 (1998): 66–71.

Diagnostic and Statistical Manual of Mental Disorders. 4th ed. (Washington, D.C.: American Psychiatric Association, 1994.)

Elia, Josephine; Ambrosini, Paul; and Rapopart, Judith. Treatment of attention-deficit/hyperactivity disorder. *New England Journal of Medicine*. 340 (1999): 780–88.

Hallowell, Edward, and Ratey, John. *Driven to Distraction*. (New York: Touchstone, 1994.)

Kollins, Scott; MacDonald, Emily; and Rush, Craig. Assessing the abuse potential of methylphenidate in nonhuman and human subjects: a review. *Pharmacology, Biochemistry, and Behavior*. 68 (2001): 611–27.

Levine, Mel. *Keeping a Head in School*. (Cambridge, MA: Educators Publishing Service, 1990.)

Pliszka, Steven; McCraken, James; and Maas, James. Catecholamines in attention-deficit/hyperactivity disorder: current perspectives. *Journal of American Academy of Child and Adolescent Psychiatry*. 35 (1996): 264–72.

Smith, Robert; and Davis, John. Comparative effects of d-amphetamine, l-amphetamine, and methylphenidate on mood in man. *Psychopharmacology*. 53 (1977): 1–12.

Chapter 2

Biederman, Joseph; Russell, Ronald; Soriano, Jennifer; Wozniak, Janet; and Faraone, Stephen. Clinical features of children with both ADHD and mania: does ascertainment source make a difference. *Journal of Affective Disorders*. 51 (1998): 101–12.

Diagnostic and Statistical Manual of Mental Disorders. 4th ed. (Washington, D.C.: American Psychiatric Association, 1994.)

Faraone, Stephen; Biederman, Joseph; Wozniak, Janet; Mundy, Elizabeth; Mennin, Douglas; and O'Donnell, Deborah. Is comorbidity with ADHD a marker for juvenile-onset mania? *Journal of the American Academy of Child and Adolescent Psychiatry.* 36 (Aug. 1997): 1046–56.

Geller, Barbara; Williams, Marlene; Zimerman, Betsy; Frazier, Jeanne; Beringer, Linda; and Warner, Kathy. Prepubertal and early adolescent bipolarity differentiate from ADHD by manic symptoms, grandiose delusions, ultra-rapid or ultradian cycling. *Journal of Affective Disorders.* 51 (1998): 81–91.

Giedd, Jay. Bipolar disorder and attention-deficit/hyperactivity disorder in children and adolescents. *Journal of Clinical Psychiatry.* 61, suppl 9 (2000): 31–34.

Papolos, Demitri, and Papolos, Janice. *The Bipolar Child.* (New York: Broadway Books, 1999.)

Papolos, Demitri, and Papolos, Janice. Bipolar Disorder and AD/HD. *Attention!* 8 (Dec. 2001): 29–33.

Pliszka, Steven; Carlson, Caryn; and Swanson, James. *ADHD with Comorbid Disorders.* (New York: Guilford Press, 1999.)

Chapter 4

Biederman, Joseph; Mick, Eric; and Faraone, Stephen. Depression in attention deficit hyperactivity disorder (ADHD) children: "true" depression or demoralization? *Journal of Affective Disorders.* 47 (1998): 113–22.

Diagnostic and Statistical Manual of Mental Disorders. 4th ed. (Washington, D.C.: American Psychiatric Association, 1994.)

Hallowell, Edward, and Ratey, John. *Driven to Distraction.* (New York: Simon and Schuster, 1994.)

Jensen, Peter; Martin, David; and Cantwell, Dennis. Comorbidity in ADHD: implications for research, practice, and DSM-V. *Journal of the American Academy of Child and Adolescent Psychiatry.* 36 (1997): 1065–80.

Pliszka, Steven; Carlson, Caryn; and Swanson, James. *ADHD with Comorbid Disorders: Clinical Assessment and Management.* (New York: Guilford Press, 1999.)

Schmidt, Kristen; Stark, Kevin; Carlson, Caryn; and Anthony, Bruno. Cognitive factors differentiating attention deficit-hyperactivity disorder with and without a comorbid mood disorder. *Journal of Consulting and Clinical Psychology.* 66 (1998): 673–79.

Seligman, Martin. *The Optimistic Child.* (New York: Houghton Mifflin, 1995.)

Tannock, Rosemary. Attention-deficit/hyperactivity disorder with anxiety disorders. In Thomas Brown, ed. *Attention-Deficit Disorders and Comorbidities in Children, Adolescents, and Adults.* (Washington, D.C.: American Psychiatric Press, 2000.)

Chapter 6

Biederman, Joseph, and Klein, Rachel. Resolved: mania is mistaken for ADHD in prepubertal children. *Journal of the American Academy of Child and Adolescent Psychiatry.* 37 (Oct. 1998): 1091–9.

Biederman, Joseph; Mick, Eric; and Faraone, Stephen. Depression in attention deficit hyperactivity disorder (ADHD) children: "true" depression or demoralization? *Journal of Affective Disorders.* 47 (1998): 113–22.

Biederman, Joseph; Mick, Eric; Prince, Jefferson; Bostic, Jeff; Wilens, Timothy; Spencer, Thomas; Wozniak, Janet; and Faraone, Stephen. Systematic chart review of the pharmacologic treatment of comorbid attention deficit hyperactivity disorder in youth with bipolar disorder. *Journal of Child and Adolescent Psychopharmacology.* 9 (4) (1999): 247–56.

DelBello, Melissa; Schwiers, Michael; Rosenberg, H. Lee; and Strakowski, Stephen. A double-blind, randomized, placebo-controlled study of quetiapine as adjunctive treatment for adolescent mania. *Journal of the American Academy of Child and Adolescent Psychiatry*. 41 (10) (2002): 1216–23.

Diagnostic and Statistical Manual of Mental Disorders. 4th ed. (Washington, D.C.: American Psychiatric Association, 1994.)

Emslie, Graham; Heiligenstien, John; Wagner, Karen; Hoog, Sharon; Ernest, Daniel; Brown, Eileen; Nilsson, Mary; and Jacobson, Jennie. Fluoxetine for acute treatment of depression in children and adolescents: a placebo-controlled, randomized clinical trial. *Journal of the American Academy of Child and Adolescent Psychiatry*. 41 (2002): 1205–15.

Emslie, Graham; Hughes, Carroll; Crismon, Lynn; Lopez, Molly; Pliszka, Steve; Toprac, Marcia; and Boemer, Christine. A feasibility study of the childhood depression medication algorithm: the Texas children's medication algorithm project (CMAP). *Journal of the American Academy of Child and Adolescent Psychiatry*. 43:5 (2004): 519–27.

Emslie, Graham, and Mayes, Taryn. Depression in children and adolescents: a guide to diagnosis and treatment. *CNS Drugs*. 11 (1999): 181–89.

Emslie, Graham; Rush, John; Weinberg, Warren; Kowatch, Robert; Hughes, Carroll; Carmody, Tom; and Rintelmann, Jeanne. A double-blind, randomized placebo-controlled trial of fluoxetine in children and adolescents with depression. *Archives of General Psychiatry*. 54 (1997): 1031–37.

Frazier, Jean; Meyer, Michele; and Biederman, Joseph. Risperidone treatment for juvenile bipolar disorder: a retrospective chart review. *Journal of the American Academy of Child and Adolescent Psychiatry*. 38 (Aug. 1999): 960–65.

Hallowell, Edward, and Ratey, John. *Driven to Distraction*. (New York: Simon and Schuster, 1994.)

Jensen, Peter; Martin, David; and Cantwell, Dennis. Comorbidity in ADHD: implications for research, practice, and DSM-V. *Journal of the American Academy of Child and Adolescent Psychiatry*. 36 (1997): 1065–80.

Kafantaris, Vivian; Dicker, Robert; Coletti, Daniel; and Kane, Jane. Adjunctive antipsychotic treatment is necessary for adolescents with psychotic mania. *Journal of Child and Adolescent Psychopharmacology.* 11 (2001): 409–13.

Keller, Martin; Ryan, Neal; Strober, Michael; Klein, Rachel; Kutcher, Stan; Birmaher, Boris; Hagino, Owen; Koplewicz, Harold; Carlson, Gabrielle; Clarke, Gregory; Emslie, Graham; Feinberg, David; Geller, Barbara; Kusumakar, Vivek; Papatheodorou, George; Sack, William; Sweeney, Michael; Wagner, Karen; Weller, Elizabeth; Winters, Nancy; Oakes, Rosemary; and McCafferty, James. Efficacy of paroxetine in the treatment of adolescent major depression: a randomized, controlled trial. *Journal of the American Academy of Child and Adolescent Psychiatry.* 40 (2001): 762–72.

March, John; Silva, Susan; Petrycki, Stephen; Curry, John; Wells, Karen; Fairbank, John; Burns, Barbara; Domino, Marisa; McNulty, Steven; Vitiello, Benedetto; and Severe, Joanne. Fluoxetine, cognitive–behavioral therapy, and their combination for adolescents with depression: treatment for adolescents with depression study (TADS) randomized controlled trial. *Journal of the American Medical Association.* 292:7 (2004): 807–20.

Pierce, Lisa, and Emslie, Graham. Fluoxetine side effects. Presented at the *42nd Annual Meeting of the American Academy of Child and Adolescent Psychiatry*; October 17–22, 1995; New Orleans, LA (Abstract).

Pliszka, Steven; Carlson, Caryn; and Swanson, James. *ADHD with Comorbid Disorders: Clinical Assessment and Management.* (New York: Guilford Press, 1999.)

Preskorn, Sheldon. Use of antidepressants with other medications. In Preskorn, Sheldon, ed., *Outpatient Management of Depression.* (Caddo, OK: Professional Communications, 1999, 179–91.)

Schmidt, Kristen; Stark, Kevin; Carlson, Caryn; and Anthony, Bruno. Cognitive factors differentiating attention deficit-hyperactivity disorder with and without a comorbid mood disorder. *Journal of Consulting and Clinical Psychology*. 66 (1998): 673–79.

Seligman, Martin. *The Optimistic Child*. (New York: Houghton Mifflin, 1995.)

Shoaf, Thomas; Emslie, Graham; and Mayes, Taryn. Childhood depression: diagnosis and treatment strategies in general pediatrics. *Pediatric Annals*. 30 (3) (2001): 130–37.

Strober, Michael; DeAntonio, Mark; Schmidt-Lackner, Susan; Freeman, Roberta; Lampert, Carlyn; and Diamond, Jane. Early childhood attention deficit hyperactivity disorder predicts poorer response to acute lithium therapy in adolescent mania. *Journal of Affective Disorders*. 51 (1998): 145–51.

Strober, Michael; Morrell, Wendy; Lampert, Carlyn; and Burroughs, Jane. Relapse following discontinuation of lithium maintenance therapy in adolescents with bipolar I illness: a naturalistic study. *American Journal of Psychiatry*. 147 (4) (1990): 457-61.

Strober, Michael; Schmidt-Lackner, Susan; Freeman, Roberta; Bower, Stacy; Lampert, Carlyn; and DeAntonio, Mark. Recovery and relapse in adolescents with bipolar affective illness: a five-year naturalistic, prospective follow-up. *Journal of the American Academy of Child and Adolescent Psychiatry*. 34 (1995): 724–31.

Tannock, Rosemary. Attention-deficit/hyperactivity disorder with anxiety disorders. In Thomas Brown, ed. *Attention-Deficit Disorders and Comorbidities in Children, Adolescents, and Adults*. (Washington, D.C.: American Psychiatric Press, 2000.)

Wagner, Karen; Birmaher, Boris; and Carlson, Gabrielle. Safety of paroxetine and imipramine in the treatment of adolescent depression. Presented at the *New Clinical Drug Evaluation Unit Program (NCDEU), 38th Annual Meeting*; June 10–13, 1998; Boca Raton, FL.

Wilens, Timothy, and Spencer, Thomas. Pharmacology of amphetamines. In: Tarter, Ralph; Ammerman, Robert; and Ott,

Peggy, eds. *Handbook of Substance Abuse: Neurobehavioral Pharmacology*. (New York: Plenum Press, 1998, 501–13.)

Chapter 7

August, Gerald; Realmuto, George; Joyce, Tamara; and Hektner, Joel. Persistence and desistance of oppositional defiant disorder in a community sample of children with ADHD. *Journal of the American Academy of Child and Adolescent Psychiatry*. 38 (1999): 1262–70.

Biederman, Joseph; Newcorn, Jeffrey; and Sprich, Susan. Comorbidity of attention deficit hyperactivity disorder with conduct, depressive, anxiety, and other disorders. *American Journal of Psychiatry*. 148 (1991): 564–77.

Biederman, Joseph; Faraone, Stephen; Milberger, Sharon; Jetton, Jennifer; Chen, Lisa; Mick, Eric; Greene, Ross; and Russell, Ronald. Is childhood oppositional defiant disorder a precursor to adolescent conduct disorder: findings from a four-year follow-up study of children with ADHD. *Journal of the American Academy of Child and Adolescent Psychiatry*. 35 (1996): 1193–204.

Diagnostic and Statistical Manual of Mental Disorders. 4th ed. (Washington, D.C.: American Psychiatric Association, 1994.)

Kewley, Geoffrey. Risperidone in comorbid ADHD and ODD/CD. *Journal of the American Academy of Child and Adolescent Psychiatry*. 38 (1999): 1327–28.

Chapter 8

Bawden, Harry; Stokes, Aidan; Camfield, Carol; Camfield, Peter; and Salisbury, Sonia. Peer relationship problems in children with Tourette's disorder or diabetes mellitus. *Journal of Child Psychology and Psychiatry*. 39 (1998): 663–68.

Carter, Alice; O'Donnell, Deborah; Schultz, Robert; Scahill, Lawrence; Leckman, James; and Pauls, David. Social and emotional adjustment in children affected with Gilles de la Tourette's syndrome: associations with ADHD and family functioning. *Journal of Child Psychology and Psychiatry.* 41 (2000): 215–23.

Clark, T.; Feehan, C.; Tinline, C.; and Vostanis, P. Autistic symptoms in children with attention deficit–hyperactivity disorder. *European Child and Adolescent Psychiatry.* 8 (1999): 50–55.

Comings, David. Attention-deficit/hyperactivity disorder with Tourette syndrome. In *Attention-Deficit Disorders and Comorbidities in Children, Adolescents, and Adults,* Thomas Brown, ed. (Washington, D.C.: American Psychiatric Press, 2000, 363–91.)

Diagnostic and Statistical Manual of Mental Disorders. 4th ed. (Washington, D.C.: American Psychiatric Association, 1994.)

Frazier, Jean; Biederman, Joseph; Bellordre, Christine; Garfield, Stacey; Geller, Daniel; Coffey, Barbara; and Faraone, Stephen V. Should the diagnosis of attention deficit/hyperactivity disorder be considered in children with pervasive developmental disorder? *Journal of Attention Disorders.* 4:4 (2001): 203–11.

Gadow, Kenneth; Sverd, Jeffrey; Sprafkin, Joyce; Nolan, Edith; and Grossman, Steven. Long-term methylphenidate therapy in children with comorbid attention-deficit hyperactivity disorder and chronic multiple tic disorder. *Archives of General Psychiatry.* 56 (1999): 330–36.

Goldstein, Sam, and Schwebach, Adam. Does ADHD occur with pervasive developmental disorder? *The ADHD Report.* 10:6 (2002): 1–5.

Handen, Benjamin; Johnson, Cynthia; and Lubetsky, Martin. Efficacy of methylphenidate among children with autism and symptoms of attention-deficit hyperactivity disorder. *Journal of Autism and Developmental Disorders.* 30 (2000): 245–55.

Klin, A.; Volkmar, F.; Schultz, R.; Pauls, D.; and Cohen, D.J. Asperger's syndrome: phenomenology, neuropsychology, and neurobiology. Paper presented at the *44th Annual Meeting of the American Academy of Child and Adolescent Psychiatry,* Oct. 1997, Toronto.

Law, Samuel, and Schachar, Russell. Do typical clinical doses of methylphenidate cause tics in children treated for attention-deficit hyperactivity disorder? *Journal of the American Academy of Child and Adolescent Psychiatry*. 38 (1999): 944–51.

Luteijn, E.F.; Serra, M.; Jackson, S.; Steenhuis, M.P.; Althaus, M.; Volkmar, F.; and Minderaa, R. How unspecified are disorders of children with a pervasive developmental disorder not otherwise specified? *European Child and Adolescent Psychiatry*. 9 (2000): 168–79.

McDougle, Christopher; Holmes, Janice; Carlson, Derek; Pelton, Gregory; Cohen, Donald; and Price, Lawrence. A double-blind placebo-controlled study of risperidone in adults with autistic disorder and other pervasive developmental disorders. *Archives of General Psychiatry*. 55 (1998): 633–41.

Pliszka, Steven; Carlson, Caryn; and Swanson, James. *ADHD with Comorbid Disorders*. (New York: Guilford Press, 1999.)

Quintana, Humberto; Birmaher, Boris; Stedge, Deborah; Lennon, Susan; Freed, Jane; Bridge, Jeffrey; and Greenhill, Larry. Use of methylphenidate in the treatment of children with autistic disorder. *Journal of Autism and Developmental Disorders*. 25 (1995): 283–94.

Roeyers, Herbert; Keymeulen, Heidi; and Buysse, Ann. Differentiating attention–deficit/hyperactivity disorder from pervasive developmental disorder not otherwise specified. *Journal of Learning Disabilities*. 31 (1998): 565–71.

Spencer, Thomas; Biederman, Joseph; Coffey, Barbara; Geller, Daniel; Wilens, Timothy; and Faraone, Stephen. The four-year course of tic disorders in boys with attention-deficit/hyperactivity disorder. *Archives of General Psychiatry*. 56 (1999): 842–47.

Spencer, Thomas; Biederman, Joseph; Harding, Margaret; O'Donnell, Deborah; Wilens, Thomas; Faraone, Stephen; Coffey, Barbara; and Geller, Daniel. Disentangling the overlap between Tourette's disorder and ADHD. *Journal of Child Psychology and Psychiatry*. 39 (1998): 1037–44.

Tanguay, Peter. Pervasive developmental disorders: a 10-year review. *Journal of the American Academy of Child and Adolescent Psychiatry.* 39:9 (2000): 1079–95.

Chapter 9

Barkley, Russell. Does stimulant medication therapy for ADHD in children predispose to later drug use? *The ADHD Report.* 11 (2003): 2–7.

Biederman, Joseph; Wilens, Timothy; Mick, Eric; Faraone, Stephen; Weber, Wendy; Curtis, Shannon; Thornell, Ayanna; Pfister, Kiffany; Jetton, Jennifer; and Soriano, Jennifer. Is ADHD a risk factor for psychoactive substance use disorders? Findings from a four-year prospective follow-up study. *Journal of the American Academy of Child and Adolescent Psychiatry.* 36 (1997): 21–29.

Biederman, Joseph; Wilens, Timothy; Mick, Eric; Spencer, Thomas; and Faraone, Stephen. Pharmacotherapy of attention-deficit/hyperactivity disorder reduces risk for substance use disorder. *Pediatrics.* 104 (1999): 20.

Brook, Judith; Whiteman, Martin; Finch, Stephen; and Cohen, Patricia. Young adult drug use and delinquency: childhood antecedents and adolescent mediators. *Journal of the American Academy of Child and Adolescent Psychiatry.* 35 (1996): 1584–92.

Burke, Jeffry; Loeber, Rolf; and Lahey, Benjamin. Which aspects of ADHD are associated with tobacco use in early adolescence? *Journal of Child Psychology and Psychiatry.* 42 (2001): 493–502.

Chilcoat, Howard, and Breslau, Naomi. Pathways from ADHD to early drug use. *Journal of the American Academy of Child and Adolescent Psychiatry.* 38 (1999): 1347–54.

Colle, M.; Rosenzweig, P.; Bianchetti, G.; Fuseau, E.; Ruffie, A.; Ruedas, E.; and Morselli, P.L. Nocturnal profile of growth hormone secretion during sleep induced by zolpidem: a double blind study in young adults and children. *Hormone Research.* 35 (1991): 30–34.

Corkum, Penny; Moldofsky, Harvey; Hogg-Johnson, Sheilah; Humphries, Tom; and Tannock, Rosemary. Sleep problems in children with attention–deficit/hyperactivity disorder: impact of subtype, comorbidity, and stimulant medication. *Journal of the American Academy of Child and Adolescent Psychiatry.* 38 (1999): 1285–93.

Gruber, Reut; Sadeh, Avi; and Raviv, Amiram. Instability of sleep patterns in children with attention–deficit/hyperactivity disorder. *Journal of the American Academy of Child and Adolescent Psychiatry.* 39 (2000): 495–501.

Jaffe, S. Failed attempts at intranasal abuse of concerta. *Journal of the American Academy of Child and Adolescent Psychiatry.* 41. (2002): 5.

Konofal, Eric; Lecendreux, Michel; Bouvard, Manuel; and Mouren-Simeoni, Marie-Christine. High levels of nocturnal activity in children with attention–deficit hyperactivity disorder: a video analysis. *Psychiatry and Clinical Neurosciences.* 55 (2001): 97–103.

Lambert, Nadine, and Hartsough, Carolyn. Prospective study of tobacco smoking and substance dependencies among samples of ADHD and non–ADHD participants. *Journal of Learning Disabilities.* 31 (1998): 533–44.

Levin, Frances, and Kleber, Herbert. Attention deficit hyperactivity disorder and substance abuse: relationships and implications for treatment. *Harvard Review of Psychiatry.* 2 (1995): 246–58.

Mick, Eric; Biederman, Joseph; Jetton, Jennifer; and Faraone, Stephen. Sleep disturbances associated with attention deficit hyperactivity disorder: the impact of psychiatric comorbidity and pharmacotherapy. *Journal of Child and Adolescent Psychopharmacolgy.* 10 (2000): 223–31.

Molina, Brooke, and Pelham, William. Childhood predictors of adolescent substance use in a longitudinal study of children with ADHD. *Journal of Abnormal Psychology.* 112 (2003): 497–507.

Molina, Brooke; Smith, Bradley; and Pelham, William. Interactive effects of attention deficit hyperactivity disorder and conduct disorder on early adolescent substance use. *Psychology of Addictive Behaviors.* 13 (1999): 348–58.

Peggs, James; Shimp, Leslie; and Opdycke, Ruth. Antihistamines: the old and the new. *American Family Physician.* 52 (1995): 593–600.

Riggs, Paula. Clinical approach to treatment of ADHD in adolescents with substance use disorders and conduct disorder. *Journal of the American Academy of Child and Adolescent Psychiatry.* 37 (1998): 331–32.

Riggs, Paula; Leon, Stacy; Mikulich, Susan; and Pottle, Laura. An open trial of bupropion for ADHD in adolescents with substance use disorders and conduct disorder. *Journal of the American Academy of Child and Adolescent Psychiatry.* 37 (1998): 1271–78.

Stein, Daniel; Pat-Horenczyk, Ruth; Blank, Shulamit; Dagan, Yaron; Barak, Yoram; and Gumpel, Thomas. Sleep disturbances in adolescents with symptoms of attention-deficit/hyperactivity disorder. *Journal of Learning Disabilities.* 35 (2002): 268–75.

Stein, Mark. Unraveling sleep problems in treated and untreated children with ADHD. *Journal of Child and Adolescent Psychopharmacology.* 9 (1999): 157–68.

Wilens, Timothy. Impact of ADHD and its treatment on substance abuse. *American Psychological Association Symposium,* August 2002.

Wilens, Timothy; Faraone, Stephen; Biederman, Joseph; and Gunawardene, Samantha. Does stimulant therapy of attention-deficit/hyperactivity disorder beget later substance abuse? A meta-analytic review of the literature. *Pediatrics.* 111 (2003): 179–85.

Index

About the Authors

David Gottlieb, Ph.D., is a licensed clinical psychologist who has worked with ADHD children and adolescents and their families for twenty years. Dr. Gottlieb has written articles for *Attention!* magazine about children who have ADHD and other emotional problems. He holds a doctorate in clinical psychology from Northwestern University and a bachelor's degree in psychology from Harvard University. Dr. Gottlieb's office is in Homewood, Illinois.

 Thomas Shoaf, M.D., M.B.A., is a board-certified psychiatrist who has served as a clinician, researcher, and faculty member at the University of Chicago and at the University of Texas Southwestern Medical Center. While assistant professor of psychiatry at the University of Chicago, Dr. Shoaf conducted research on medication for pediatric psychiatric illnesses and also served as medical director of the Sonia Shankman Orthogenic School, a residential treatment facility for children and adolescents. He has published articles in several medical journals. He earned his undergraduate degree at Stanford University in human biology and his medical degree at the University of Kansas Medical School. He completed his residency and child and adolescent psychiatry fellowship at the University of Texas Southwestern Medical Center at Dallas. Dr. Shoaf also completed his M.B.A. at Kellogg Graduate School of Management, Northwestern University, and presently works in clinical development in the pharmaceutical industry.

 Risa Graff, M.A., BCET, is a board-certified educational therapist who uses a combination of intensive and individualized educational, remedial, and therapeutic approaches to help students develop self-awareness and overcome attention and learning difficulties. She has developed her methods through thirty years of private practice and in coaching her own three children. Graff is a third-degree black belt and certified tae kwon do teacher who calls upon techniques from martial arts, yoga, and games to teach her students how to put their brains on "high power." She received a master's degree in education of the hearing impaired from Northwestern University and a bachelor's degree in learning disabilities and elementary education from the University of Illinois at Chicago. Her office is in Olympia Fields, Illinois.